Teach Your Kids...
Bean's About Baseball

Copyright © March 1994 by Kenneth W. Bean

Cover Photo by © Ronald C. Modra - **Sports Illustrated**

Library of Congress Cataloging-in-Publication
Data: 92-062244

Bean, Kenneth

Teach Your Kids...
BEAN'S ABOUT BASEBALL
ISBN: 0-9634557-8-8

OBL Publishing Corporation
8966 Wilcrest Dr.
Houston, Texas 77099
(713) 569-3896

Printed in The United States of America

About the Author

Bean played baseball at the collegiate level. Awarded a scholarship to pitch for Baylor University, he was farmed out to Panola Jr. College first. He lettered on a team that had been a national finalist the year before, pitching to an All American catcher.

He discovered very quickly that he did not have the physical gifts to compete at the college level, but attained some success by diligently studying and practicing the components of the game.

Having majored in Family counseling at Baylor, he spent five years in the profession before translating his skills into the business world. He was named U.S. President of a Japanese multi-national trading company while still in his twenties.

Mr. Bean lives in Houston, a business consultant, writer, public speaker, and little league coach. When asked about champions he has coached, he hands you his team rosters and tells you:

"Every one of these youngsters".

To my son,
John Christian,
who has taught me
so much

Table of Contents

CHAPTER ONE:
Playing To Win 1

CHAPTER TWO:
Hitting The Line Drive 7

1. "The Grip", "The Stance", "The Bat Ready",
   "The Wrist Roll", "The Stride", "Body English",
   and "The Head In"
2. A Note On Bunting
3. A Note On Fear

CHAPTER THREE:
Catching A Ball 35

1. A Good Glove
2. Starting From Scratch: The Mirror Drill
3. The Concept Of "Between Forefinger
   And Thumb"
4. Pop Flys And Grounders
5. The Float: Running With His Heels
   Off The Ground
6. Use Two Hands? No Way, Dad!

CHAPTER FOUR:
Throwing The Ball 49

1. The Grip
2. Start Sideways
3. Good Drills

CHAPTER FIVE:
Playing The Outfield 59

1. The Outfield Is **NOT** Siberia
2. The Outfielders Win Games
3. Kick It, Stomp It, Bite It, But Don't Let It
   Get Past You

CHAPTER SIX:
Playing The Infield 69
1. Charge Every Ball
2. Notes On The Positions
3. Hit Sharply: Force The Lead Runner, Hit Softly,
   Get Him At First

CHAPTER SEVEN:
The Batteries 79
1. The Pitcher And Catcher Are A Team
2. They Win or Loose Together

CHAPTER EIGHT:
Base Running: Sliding Is The Fastest Way To Stop 93
1. Turn Those Bases
2. A "HOOK SLIDE" A Day Keeps The
   Doctor Away

PART TWO: TEAM MANAGER'S SECTION

CHAPTER NINE: ·
Practice For Winners 109
1. Setting The Tone
2. Having Some Fun
3. A Contract With Parents
4. Two Practice Plans
5. Pre-Game Practice

CHAPTER TEN:
Pitcher and Catcher Practice 131

CHAPTER ELEVEN:
Conclusions and Coach's "CUES" 141

CHAPTER ONE

Playing To Win

The forms, drills, and techniques
presented in this book are TIME-TESTED
and KID-TESTED.* THEY WORK!

The book's title suggests its focus: Beans, Meat, and Potatoes—fundamental staples the kids will use every day. I have declined the temptation of fluffing up the work with big league refinements or alternative methods of dubious value. Too many teachers seem to focus on trying to teach young players about the fine wines and caveats of baseball they will enjoy only occasionally, even when they are much older.

Then there is that ENORMOUS HEAP of mis-information, myth, and cliche being perpetuated year after year after year. Most of it is passed along by well-meaning people, but the end result is that the kids are sent out on a baseball field without the proper tools for success. Worse, some of that misinformation is down-right dangerous!

With this book, you can give your kids the tools that won't fail them:

> * PROVEN TECHNIQUES
> * FUN DRILLS TO FIRMLY IMPLANT THE TECHNIQUES
> * VERBAL "CUES" FOR REINFORCING THE TECHNIQUES

In addition, I will be striving to persuade you parents and coaches to imbue your kids with "A WINNER'S PERSPECTIVE". You have that wonderful power to define "winner" for your children, and using your own words, it will mean something like "Be the best YOU can be."

A WINNER:

1. If you did your best, YOU WON!

2. Baseball is a team sport. If your TEAM wins, YOU WIN!

3. The scoreboard only tells which team scored more runs on a particular day. It does NOT indicate your value to the universe.

4. Scoring more runs is the object of the contest, but NO TEAM scores more runs every game.

5. When you make a mistake, you are allowed ONE PRIMAL SCREAM. Then put the mistake behind you. Try to understand how you goofed up and try not to repeat it...too often.

6. With practice, your best will become a lot better, BUT DON'T EVER PRACTICE SLOPPILY. The object of practicing is to make doing it right a muscular memory.

7. Always be supportive of your teammates, especially when they make an honest mistake.

Now we can proceed to discuss the four elements which constitute the "WINNER'S PERSPECTIVE". They are:

> * CONFIDENCE
> * SOUND MOTIVATION
> * CONCENTRATION
> * EMOTION.

I must digress here, dad or mom, to congratulate you. The very fact that you've read this far speaks well of YOUR motivation.

CONFIDENCE is NOT something a child can be talked into or conned into. It can only be real. It can only be built on success and based on success. Our task is to recognize their small successes with some heart-felt "atta-boygurls", and do so, often! Their confidence will grow.

SOUND MOTIVATION is a quite illusive concept. A lot of misinformed parents and coaches out there still believe that a person can "be motivated", like filling a gas tank with gasoline or something. Nothing could be further from the truth!

Every single human being alive has motivations already. We simply encourage the healthy ones. Perhaps the prime motivation for preadolescent children is their desire for recognition and approval from their parents and peers. (There's those "atta-boygurls" again.)

CONCENTRATION is merely an application of mental self-discipline. Some pretty perceptive person back in the mists of sports history called it, "PUTTING ON YOUR GAME FACE". This is a prime example of the verbal CUES I spoke about earlier. "The Face" is an excellent physical construct supporting a mental attitude.

EMOTION is without any question the most powerful force on earth. Every single accomplishment, and every single tragedy in human history is based on it.

We need to reinforce the positive emotions among the kids, and among ourselves as dads and coaches: the joy of success, the desire for recognition, the hope for approval, and regard for the feelings and aspirations of our rivals.

We also need to accept the sometimes painful reality of our limitations coupled with the resolve to do our best.

Finally, this is a book about "Father-love", defined as a love that stretches our kids to reach ever higher while building a trust that we will always be there right behind them, cheering them on.

They need to experience the ongoing reality that win or lose...success or bitter defeat...we're on their side!

This is the relationship that will endure through those tough teen years, and organized baseball is a wonderful vehicle for us grown-ups to demonstrate our unqualified support of a good effort.

Too, baseball is a remarkable reflection of the best in our society; opportunities for teamwork AND individual achievement, a working knowledge of the spirit of fair play, and perhaps most important, a good start on practicing that fine balance between spirited competition and honorable cooperation that makes America the envy of the world.

* A NOTE ABOUT GIRLS

There is no intention whatsoever in this book to overlook or disparage girls. They have hopes and dreams and needs too, but the vast majority of girls I've known have been conditioned long before baseball-playing age to approach the world a little differently than boys.

I don't have any experience teaching girls to play baseball. If I had a daughter, from the time she was old enough to wear clothes I would have had her in jeans and sneakers as often as in frilly dresses and hair ribbons, and I would have taken her fishing, camping, and ball-playing.

I would have played rough and tumble with her, too, just the same as I give my son lots of hugs and affection.

If some of you parents out there feel as I do and want your girl to play baseball, then read the book with her and mark out every textual "him" and "he" and write in "girl" and "she". Make a big deal out of it and prove to her that she is important and capable in your eyes.

Also, except for the grip on the ball, and underhanded pitching mechanics which I am totally unqualified to teach, the techniques in the book have proven remarkably effective for Softball coaches who got a copy of our 1993 limited release edition.

Hitting The Line Drive

The prime element in baseball is hitting a thrown ball with a stick. Though you may not believe it yet, any kid can do it, unless he is profoundly handicapped, and he can do it consistently and well.

All he needs is a simple set of tools: THE GRIP, THE STANCE, THE BAT READY POSITION, THE WRIST ROLL, THE STRIDE, BODY ENGLISH, AND HEAD POSITION.

Since the mists of pre-history, every human being who ever picked up a club to hit something probably gripped that club the same way. Unfortunately, that instinctive grip was used for an over-hand swing. Our earliest ancestors probably developed that over-hand swing to whack rabbits or saber-toothed tigers or something. Later, that over-hand swing was perfected during thousands of years of chopping wood and hoeing crops.

That instinctive grip simply will not work very well when someone attempts the horizontal swing needed to hit a thrown baseball, though.

IT JUST WON'T DO!

Hitting a line drive consistently requires a slashing reflexive swing without hitches or muscularly-induced variations, to simply ALLOW hand and eye cooperation. WITHOUT THE PROPER GRIP, EVERYTHING ELSE IS WASTED.

The best drill I have discovered for the kids to achieve consistency is that each time they get ready to swing at a pitch, they rest the tip of their bat on the ground, LOOSEN THEIR GRIP, and move their fore-arms together until they are one directly above the other. Only then do they tighten their grip and move the bat to the ready position.

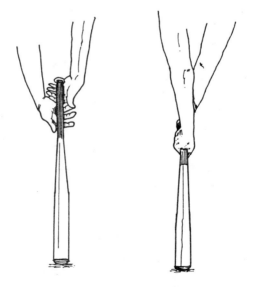

The verbal "CUE" I use to remind them is: "POINTY KNUCKLES...POINTY KNUCKLES!"

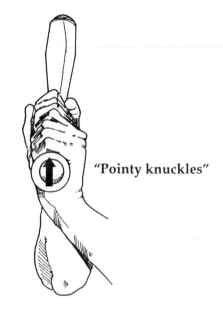

"Pointy knuckles"

If you don't think "THE GRIP" is going to feel weird to them the first thousand swings or so, try it yourself. Your very genes will **scream** to you that you are doing it wrong!

In fact, unless you are a golfer or played baseball through the collegiate level, chances are no one ever taught **you**, and it will feel awkward as the dickens.

If you ceased playing baseball in your early teens as so many do, and if you weren't such a great hitter then, go find a batting cage with a pitching machine and discover just what you missed before reading any further. BE ESPECIALLY SURE YOU UNDERSTAND THIS PERFECTLY BEFORE YOU SHOW IT TO THE KIDS.

THE BAT-READY POSITION

This step in getting ready to hit a ball is closely related to "THE GRIP". THE BATTER'S REAR ELBOW MUST BE HIGHER THAN HIS FRONT ELBOW! In fact, you will know that rear elbow is high enough only if that REAR upper arm is <u>EXACTLY HORIZONTAL</u>.

If he maintains the proper grip, his rear elbow up will force his front elbow, (and shoulder), DOWN. Almost every line drive he will ever see hit begins right here, but a lot of batters he sees will start lower and <u>hitch back</u> first. We are simply removing the hitch.

Your students' hands will almost inevitably slip around the bat to the old comfortable "rabbit-whacking" grip as they raise the bat to the "READY POSITION". You must monitor them constantly until they get used to the bent back wrists that accompany the RIGHT grip.

**Note the hands in
close to the chest
for leverage.
Very important!"**

Since every human body is constructed the same way, this "FULL-COCK" bat-ready position allows your batter to make the correct swing. (The correct swing will resemble a right cross thrown by a boxer, NOT to be confused with a right hook.) The rear hand will be "punching" straight toward the pitcher.

Without this starting place, it's virtually an accident if he does make the swing correctly. In addition, this starting place takes the attractiveness away from swinging at pitches above the armpits. CHASING HIGH PITCHES JUST WON'T BE AS MUCH FUN ANYMORE!

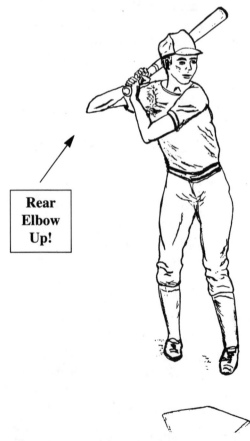

**Rear
Elbow
Up!**

Art Howe, Manager of the Houston Astros, was kind enough to give me a critical review of the book, and questioned my deletion of the what I term the "hitch-back". He pointed out that most hitting coaches around the country teach the "hitch-back" as a timing device and a dynamic coiling of the muscles as an intregal part of the swing.

There is no question at all that starting lower and hitching back as the stride begins in a sort of scissoring motion is the ideal form, but I have not been able to teach it succesfully to the vast majority of kids aged twelve and under. It might be the 46 foot pitching distance that is the problem, or perhaps most kids in this age group simply haven't consolidated their whole-body reflexes yet.

What ever the case may actually be, I **have** been able to succesfully teach the "full cock" starting position to virtually every child in my care with wonderful results for them. At the same time, when the kids make the transition to the larger diamond, I do recommend that you begin feeding in the idea of the scissoring motion. By that time, chances are your kid's muscular memory of the "BAT READY POSITION" you will have taught him can evolve into his "FIRING-POINT" WITHOUT DETRACTING FROM THE ADVANTAGES HE HAS ALREADY GAINED FROM THE "FULL-COCK" TAUGHT HERE.

Mr. Howe did point out very carefully that the "hitch-back" should not be exagerated, but only a hands-movement of perhaps three to five inches back to that ideal "firing-point", or what I have described as the "full cock".

Dad, please don't jump in the car and rush down to the batting cage with your ten year old to start working on the "SCISSORS". He's a great kid, but he is still growing and he needs the starting place I have taught thoroughly ingrained for a solid foundation. Please wait at least until he turns twelve before you start complicating things for him.

While a lot of other dads and coaches are busy screaming at their youngsters to mimic big lea-guers in every way, yours will be busy driving the ball deep and listening to your cheers.

There is only ONE more thing to remember. They MUST point the tip of their bat toward third base,* and they must keep it there until they begin their swing. CUE: **"THE FULL COCK."**

The bat should be pointed slightly above the horizontal with a <u>small</u> rotational movement to prevent muscle-lock. (CUE PHRASE: "COCK YOUR GUN NOW!")

*The bat tip should be pointed toward first base if the kid bats left-handed, and he almost certainly should if he is left-handed, thus properly utilizing his dominant eye.

A NOTE ON BAT SELECTION

BAT CONTROL AND **BAT-SPEED** ARE THE CRU-
CIAL INGREDIENTS TO HITTING WITH POWER,
NOT BAT WEIGHT OR LENGTH. Your kids will
almost always pick out a bat that is a lot heavier and
longer than they can handle, and your tendency will be to
go along with them since you will think, "OK, the kid can
grow up to the bat and I won't have to buy another one
next year." Mom and dad, we aren't talking about blue-
jeans here. I've seen eight year old kids kids come out to
the first practice with a bat that I would have a hard time
swinging in live play.

If you don't have access to a batting cage with a selection
of bats to experiment with, a quick and dirty method of
sizing the bat is to go to a store that has a pretty good
selection, WITH THE KID. Have him hold the bat with
one hand, and next to the knob, horizontally at arms
reach. If his face turns red or the veins in your daughter's
neck stand out and she starts trembling and perspiring...
THAT BAT IS PROBABLY TOO BIG!

What you want is the heaviest and longest bat that your
kids can hold extended horizontally, AND COMFORT-
ABLY WAGGLE UP AND DOWN WITH ONLY
THEIR WRIST.

If in live play the bat proves slightly too heavy, having
them "choke-up" by moving both hands up the bat an
inch or two will suffice.

THE WRIST ROLL

When swinging at a thrown ball, THE GRIP we spent so much time studying allows a wonderful thing to happen. Instead of being HANDCUFFED, our batter can roll his rearward wrist over the front wrist, ACCELERATING THE BAT-HEAD TO UNBELIEVABLE SPEEDS.

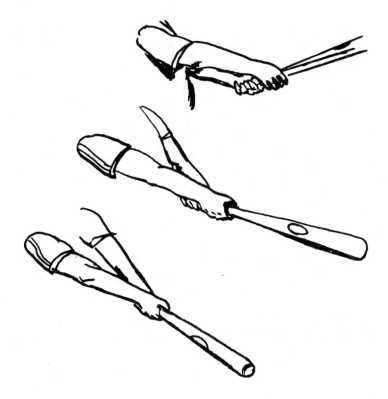

In years past it was called "buggy-whipping it", but that phrase has lost its meaning in these days for obvious reasons. Let's just call it a "WRIST-ROLL". I have been personally delighted watching the scrawniest, littlest kids on my teams <u>consistently</u> driving line shots through the holes and deep into the outfield, and they do it with the "Wrist-Roll".

Our batter doesn't have to loosen his grip to do it either, or let go of the bat, because our magic grip will allow that roll to happen about half-way through the swing, WITH NO HOP IN THE SWING, forced loosening of a hand, or the inevitable slowing of the bat due to his hands being locked up with "hand-cuffs".

Dad, its really something beautiful to see; almost as beautiful as the smile on your kid's face the first few times he "cranks one" in a game when his team is counting on him.

The WRIST ROLL allows a lot of other exciting things to happen also, but most important, it allows the kid to follow through with the swing, DRIVING THE BAT THROUGH THE BALL. In fact, done properly the swing will end with the bat almost touching his back, even after driving through that ball.

So, with "THE GRIP" and rolling the wrists, the bat-head begins accelerating from the moment the swing begins and <u>reaches its highest speed about the time the bat is pointing at first base.</u>

That is <u>precisely</u> the reason a batter gets his best power when he <u>pulls</u> the ball to left field, (or right field if he bats left handed). You can see from the diagram the geometry involved.

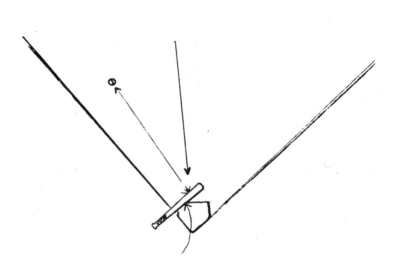

An excellent drill to help the kids achieve their best power is to use a batting tee. Place the tee WELL IN FRONT of the plate with the ball positioned in front of the inside corner. This gets them used to the idea of hitting the inside pitch, since it is the only one they can hit with full power.

An even better exercise is the "SOFT-TOSS DRILL."

Put your batter in the stance we will shortly discuss, and kneel down so that your nose is about four feet from the arc of the bat tip, just outside the foul line across from him. Now with a soft underhanded motion, toss the ball into the strike-zone and let the kid hit away. You will toss the balls well out in front of the plate to mimic an inside corner pitch, and over the plate itself to mimic where contact is ALWAYS made with an outside pitch.

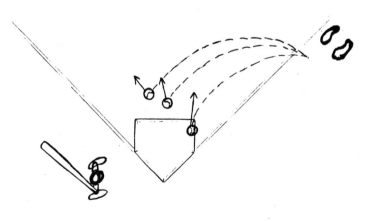

By tossing the balls in a head-high arc you can mimic a slow pitch, and by tossing them with hardly any arc at all, you can mimic a very fast pitch.

This drill not only gets the kids used to swinging effectively at pitches all over the strike zone, it is a great diagnostic tool.

As you begin the underhanded tossing motion the student will anticipate the "pitch" and react much as he would to a "live pitch". If he "breaks form", (by dropping his hands for a looping swing or other undesirable habits), you can abort the underhanded toss motion and begin reprogramming his muscular memories, <u>right then!</u>

THE STANCE: CLOSED!

There are a lot of theories about this subject, and several of them are excellent. I have opted for the method that is superior in every respect. It is especially good for the kids from ages 6 to 12 to learn because it can be easily refined as they get older and have to face curve balls, and have grown taller and stronger.

Another advantage of the CLOSED STANCE is that it affords them protection from being hit in the belly or the face with a thrown ball. Since they are positioned facing slightly away from the pitcher, their own reflexes take control when trying to avoid being hit. THEY AUTOMATICALLY TURN THEIR BACK ON THE UNAVOIDABLE WILD PITCH, and walk away with nothing worse than a small sting on their backside.

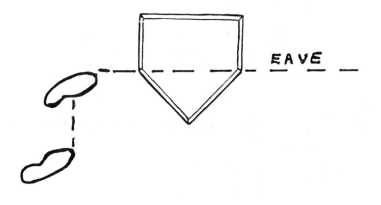

EAVE

As you can see, BOTH of the batter's feet are pointed **slightly** toward the pitcher and the batter's front foot is **even** with the "eave of the home".

Some well-meaning coaches advise the student to move back toward the catcher to gain some reaction time if they are swinging late. This strategy has several short-comings, the first of which is that moving back three feet makes a negligible difference. Second, it detracts from solving the problem at the source.

CHRONIC LATE SWINGS ARE CAUSED BY SWINGING TOO MUCH BAT!

The solution is simple. Swing <u>less</u> bat, either by choking-up, (which changes the leverage ratio), or swapping bats.

"STRIKING DISTANCE"

If it were not so devastating to our childrens' efforts, watching them take their stance merely in the same County with home plate would provoke a chuckle. For some reason, most kids seem content if they are in the right general vicinity. I must tell you though; EVEN AN <u>INCH OF INCONSISTENCY</u> HERE WILL COST YOUR BATTERS 20% OF THEIR BASE-HITS.

A good drill to teach proper distance from the plate is to have the batters put their front toe adjacent to the "eave" of the home, (plate), scratch a mark behind that heel with their other foot, and then place their front foot toe adjacent to that mark, ONE OF <u>THEIR</u> FOOT LENGTHS from the plate. With this precision they are achieving THREE crucial objectives.

First, with consistent position they learn what a ball in the strike-zone always looks like. Second, they are getting their concentration centered in the batters box and establishing a comfort level there. Third, their ability to time their swing takes a quantum leap.

Alright. Our batter is properly stationed in a closed stance, (which means that his back foot toe is FIVE inches further from the plate than his front toe), with feet spaced A LITTLE CLOSER TOGETHER than feels comfortable, (about "shoulder-width"). Now let's get him to put the majority of his weight on his BACK foot. Sometimes it helps if you instruct him to lift his front foot heel slightly off the ground. That way his hips automatically shift toward the catcher and his weight shifts with them.

You will get some delightfully funny comments as the kids go through these contortions the first few times. Relax and enjoy it. Humor is sometimes the best way to wean them from bad habits or bad inclinations.

THE STRIDE...

...IS MADE SO THAT THE FRONT FOOT COMES DOWN WITH THE TOE POINTED STRAIGHT AT THE PITCHER!

The second most important thing to remember is not to let the kids stride too far, OR TOO HEAVILY as they swing. Not to worry. If in batting practice they hit pop-fly balls instead of the desired LINE DRIVES, simply get them to shorten that stride a little. If they are doing everything else we have discussed properly, that is the only adjustment they will need to make.

A stride of about four to six inches will be about right. If they continually hit CHOPPERS, (bouncing grounders), get them to lengthen their stride an inch or two.

IT IS ABSOLUTELY CRUCIAL THAT THEY KEEP THEIR WEIGHT ON THEIR <u>BACK</u> FOOT DURING THE STRIDE, KEEPING THEIR WEIGHT <u>BEHIND</u> THE BAT, IN ORDER TO ACCELERATE THE BAT-HEAD OUT AHEAD OF THEM!

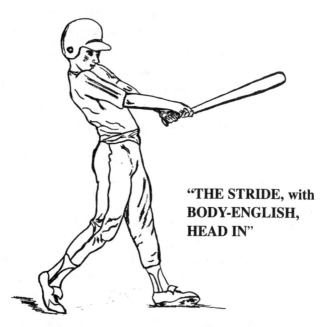

"THE STRIDE, with BODY-ENGLISH, HEAD IN"

If they transfer their weight to their front foot too early, they will be dragging the bat through the "hitting arc" behind them instead of accelerating the bat-head out in front of them.

A great idea for instilling the concept came from a YMCA sports director. He talked about having the kids "<u>Pat</u> your front foot down like a musician keeping time to the music. Don't **stomp** that front foot down! Hit the ball on the down-beat!"

Note: Your kids will see big leaguers with an extremely wide stance and hardly any stride at all. They simply lift their front knee and then put their foot back down in the same place. This is due to the breaking pitches they have to face. Breaking pitches are almost impossible to throw from the 46 feet common to leagues for kids 12 and under though, and most 13 and 14 year olds don't have much more than a "wrinkle" anyway, even though they are pitching the full 60 feet.

BODY ENGLISH:

For lack of a better term, I use this CUE to talk about rotating one's hips toward the pitcher during the stride.

This drill can be a lot of fun, (if embarrassing to non-baseballers). Get the kids to stand in the proper relationship to the plate, swing and stride, AND <u>THRUST</u> THEIR HIPS TOWARD THE PITCHER AT THE SAME TIME. Their front toe will turn <u>to point straight at the pitcher</u>!

They will naturally be lifting their rear heel off the ground in this process, as their <u>rear **HEEL** pivots **AWAY** from the pitcher!</u> "Planting" and pivoting with most of their weight on that rear toe is how they get SERIOUS power into their swing at no extra cost. They will have just enough weight on their front foot to provide balance.

(That is why you will see great power hitters with their front foot turning over to its outside edge. There is not enough weight on that front foot to overcome the tremendous torque generated by their "body-english").

THE HEAD IN: (Keeping one's eye on the ball)

Instruct your budding Mickey Mantles in one last technique. Tell them to watch the ball from the instant of the pitcher's release, and right on through the shock of the ball hitting their bat.

A concept that <u>must</u> be gotten across is that for a ball to go through the rather large invisible rectangle that we call the "strike-zone" there at the plate, IT MUST FIRST GO THROUGH A VERY SMALL RECTANGLE ABOUT TWO FEET IN FRONT OF A PITCHER'S RELEASE-POINT. Your batters must recognize a pitch coming through that <u>small</u> rectangle.

(See the picture on the next page.)

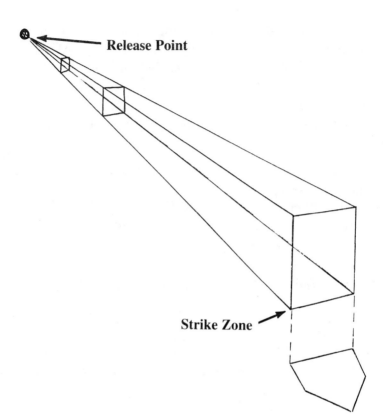

Release Point

Strike Zone

Caution them NEVER to look at the pitcher's face or his wind-up, but only the ball. Tell them to watch the ball even while the pitcher is futzing around on the mound prior to throwing. It trains their eye to begin focusing on the ball at that distance. CUE: "KEEP YOUR HEAD IN AND WATCH THE RELEASE!"

You will see your kids improve dramatically from the very first session of implementing these principles and techniques. With a little work and experimentation they will add AT LEAST two hundred points to their batting average this season!

In fact, you can make this promise to them from me: "We are going to teach you to be one of those "<u>SCAREY</u>" hitters that make infielders wish they could dig a fox-hole when you come to the plate!"

A NOTE ON BUNTING, OR:

HOW TO CATCH A BALL ON YOUR BAT!

Again, as in everything in baseball there are a lot of theories and methods out there. The method I propose to you is simple to explain and demonstrate...and accomplish. ITS NOT FANCY! IT JUST WORKS! And when you NEED a bunt you REALLY need it!

1. Square around, EARLY, (as the pitcher lifts his arms to deliver), AND COMPLETELY, and point both feet directly at the pitcher. The foot nearest the plate should be about six inches from the plate.

2. With knees bent, A LOT, SO THAT YOUR BAT-TERS' EYES ARE ALMOST LEVEL WITH THE TOP OF THE STRIKE ZONE, teach them to hold the bat out level so that their eyes are PEEKING over the top of the bat at the ball release.

3. Arms should be AT FULL EXTENSION LESS THAN LOCKED. I cannot stress too strongly that the bat must be well out front of the batter. Their arms should be slightly bent, but just the tiniest bit.

4. The bat grip shouldn't change ONE IOTA from their normal grip except that they slide their top hand up the bat about **twelve inches**. Their top hand will now be centered on the edge of the bat's rubber grip. Teach your bunters to grip the bat very firmly with both hands.

Art Howe expressed some concern with my advice to teach the kids to wrap their hand around the bat with their upper hand while laying down a bunt. He spoke about balls "tailing in" or "breaking in" on their fingers. Since this is the last teaching guide you may ever read, I must caution you here.

Though thrown balls won't tail or break much from 46 foot pitching distance common to leagues for children under twelve, they most certainly can, AND WILL, as your child gets older and moves up to the larger diamond.

THEREFORE: THE ABSOLUTELY SAFEST WAY TO GRIP THE BAT WHILE BUNTING IS "THE PINCH BETWEEN THUMB AND <u>BENT</u> FOREFINGER" FOR THE UPPER HAND.

Most children simply cannot control the bat precisely enough with this method though, or grip that bat firmly enough to roll the bunt far enough to be effective. They usually end up trying to "punch" the bunt which usually results in a pop-up or a missed ball.

If you do decide to teach "the full hand wrap" demonstrated here, then practice it a lot so your children get used to moving the bat left and right, and up and down, WHILE KEEPING THAT BAT AS HORIZONTAL AS POSSIBLE!

5. You have just taught them to lay down the perfect bunt, STRAIGHT BACK TO THE PITCHER WHICH WILL GET THEM PUT OUT! SO...

Now, having them keep everything else constant, show them how to pull the BOTTOM hand back toward them about 3 inches, and to LOCK the angle. If the bunter is a right handed batter that angle will place the bunt on the grass on the third base line. DON'T LET THEM PUNCH THE BUNT! REMIND THEM THAT THEY ARE "CATCHING THE BALL ON THE BAT". The firm grip will roll the ball far enough.

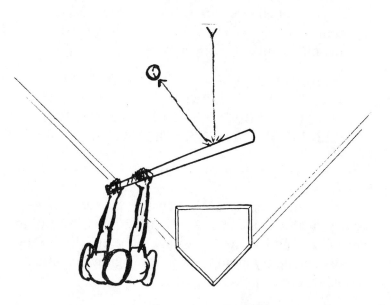

A NOTE ON FEAR:

When you stop and think about it, standing within a foot or so of a fifty mile per hour missile and trying to deflect it with a stick is not a very rational thing to do. Compound that essential reality with the fact that the person hurling that missile frequently has only a general idea of where it's going to go.

Fear and caution is the only **intelligent** response, and the "fight or flight" syndrome WILL come into play. Cajole your kids into the former and you have half the battle won. Make it a DARE! Kids have been indulging in dares since time began.

The not so obvious place to end this discussion is with the exercise you should practice FIRST. I've saved the best for last.

Put your kids in a closed batting stance, step back fifteen (15) long paces, AND START TOSSING BALLS AT THEM! You want to use soft rubber type balls of course, and make them wear a helmet. When a particular child quits diving in the dirt and begins to laugh at your failure to hit him, tell him you are switching to real baseballs. THEY STING!

(There are soft skinned balls out there now that look exactly like real ones too.) Now ask him how far the ball has to miss him not to hurt. (That's right, just a little.)

The kids will respect real baseballs more, but pretty soon they will know TWO things; THEY STING, BUT ONLY FOR A MINUTE! THEY WILL ALSO BE EXPERT DODGERS FROM THEIR <u>CLOSED</u> STANCE AND WILL STOP WORRYING ABOUT IT.

The overriding argument for teaching the **"closed"** batting stance is that it provides the best method of getting out of a thrown ball's path.

If your batters take a "square stance" or "straight-away" stance where their feet are in direct line with a pitch, the only way they can dodge is to **<u>fall</u>** away from a pitch, depending on gravity to pull them out of the way in time. **<u>GRAVITY ACTS SLOWLY!</u>**

By placing their feet slightly **<u>out</u>** of line with a pitch, they can **<u>PUSH</u>** themselves perpendicularly to the pitch **VERY VERY QUICKLY.**

Once your players discover just how fast they can get out of the way, two great things happen. First, their confidence in their ability to "duck" will skyrocket. Second, they will actually have more time to watch a pitch with the intent of hitting it, before they must start deciding on whether they need to "bail-out".

CONCLUSION

Perhaps the two most over-used and misleading cliches in baseball are, respectively:

> 1. "JUST MEET THE BALL!"

> 2. "MAKE THE <u>LEVEL</u> SWING!"

Let me lay the first one to rest by saying that "meeting the ball" will never produce anything but tentative swings that make outs...period. Teach **your** kids to swing with confident authority.

Second, the entire "strike-zone" in baseball is **below** where all the great hitters have their hands when they start their swing. Every one of them slash **downward** through the ball.

The perfect swing in baseball is **not** the sweeping swing used in golf, but a **punching** swing where the bat suddenly switches ends. The follow-through is in fact a **recoil or rebound** from the intended point of impact with the ball...**CRACKING THE WHIP!**

HAVE FUN!

Catching A Ball

Learning to catch a ball in a baseball glove is always a challenge. It ranks right up there with shoe-lace-tieing in the Developmental Task department. Most kids learn wrong to start with and are hampered ever after.

A good starter glove will seem SLIGHTLY too large. Don't get an outfield bulldozer, but don't buy the smallest one on the shelf either. Find one with soft leather. Sometimes the cheaper gloves are better because they are lighter and softer. The leather is not so dense and is rather puffy. Those gloves won't last very long, but the kids will outgrow them in a couple of years anyway. (No plastic Please!)

> For a six to eight year old, the glove should measure 8 to 9 inches from top of the web to the bottom of the hinge. Around age ten or eleven the kids can handle a glove at 10 to 11 inches.

Find a glove with a loose flexible web with lots of gaps. Some of the monstrosities around these days have a web that would make a great garden spade but will never break in as a baseball glove.

Look closely to determine that the glove has a well-designed hinge on the outside heel, again for flex purposes, and then sit in front of the T.V. or something and yank that hinge back and forth with a "washing cloth between your knuckles" motion about a zillion times.

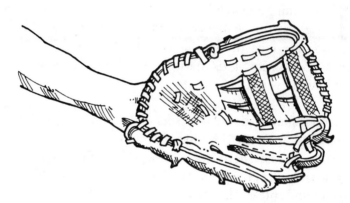

THE FIRST FINGER ON EVERY GLOVE IS ONLY A SPACER! GET YOUR KIDS TO MOVE THEIR FINGERS OVER AS FAR AS THEY CAN TOWARD THE LITTLE FINGER. NOT ONLY WILL THIS SAVE THEIR HANDS A LOT OF GRIEF, THE HAND CLOSING MOTION YOU WANT THEM TO ACHIEVE IS THAT OF FINGERS TO THUMB, NOT FINGERTIPS TO PALM. MORE ON THIS LATER.

If your ball players are five or six, (and you are to be commended for starting them out early and correctly), begin throwing to them softly under-handed. Throw the

ball so that they can catch it about knee-high CEN-
TERED. The reason for the low throws is that they are
going to try to catch it as if they are using a skillet anyway. At least make that the right move.

When a child begins to enjoy some success, begin aiming
slightly to the left and right and still knee high. As their
confidence grows, gradually aim higher and higher, BUT
ALWAYS TO THEIR LEFT AND RIGHT AT COM-
FORTABLE ARMS REACH! Don't try to go higher than
slightly below waist high during the first few sessions,
and avoid throwing directly at their body anywhere
above knee high.

All right. Now we can move along to some more
advanced drills and concepts. The best ball-catching drill
I've discovered is the MIRROR DRILL.

Before every session of playing catch, FACE YOUR
STUDENT FIVE PACES AWAY, and spend a couple of
minutes snapping your glove around briskly to the vari-
ous "catch positions": left to right, up and down, and at
arms reach and close to your body. Let your students mirror your moves as quickly as they can react.

THEIR TENDENCY WILL BE TO SHOW YOU THE
TIPS OF THEIR FINGERS, OR SHOW YOU THE
BACK OF THEIR GLOVE. HAVE THEM SHOW YOU
THE POCKET INSTEAD, WITH THE GLOVE
STRETCHED WIDE OPEN. Most books show exactly
those WRONG tendencies in their pictures.

MAKE SURE YOU AND YOUR YOUNGSTERS
BOTH DEFINE THE POCKET THE SAME WAY. IT IS
THE POINT AT THE EXACT BOTTOM CENTER OF
THE WEB.

THE MIRROR DRILL

That definition is very important to make extremely clear because our next step is to impress on them that they should "TRY TO CATCH THE BALL BETWEEN YOUR FORE-FINGER AND THUMB!" That one simple but subtle concept firmly imbedded in your students' minds will improve their catching a thousand percent.

Get your kids to take off that glove and place a ball between their forefinger and thumb. Now have them present the heel of their hand to you, (as you stand in front of them), fore-finger and thumb vertical with the other fingers spread wide. "AND THAT, GUYS, IS HOW TO CATCH A BALL IN A <u>GLOVE!</u>" you will repeat about a hundred times.

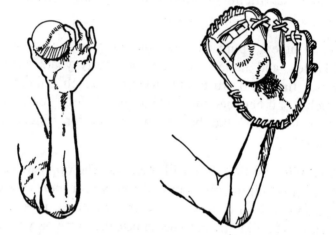

This exercise flies in the face of one of those worthless cliche's we talked about earlier. Youngsters have been taught to cup their throwing hand over the ball on every catch for as long as any of us can remember. The concept is usually articulated with a red face and an angry shout after the child has dropped a catchable ball. "Use Two hands, Dummie!" (Not Good!)

The truth is, for a long time using two hands was a **MUST**. Baseball gloves resembled a padded work glove and catching a ball ON one of them without using the opposite hand was nearly impossible. Some years ago someone had the bright idea that stringing the glove-fingers together and building in a web large enough to cup a ball would make a fielder's glove almost efficient as a first baseman's "trapper" when catching an airborne ball, without sacrificing the ground-ball-catching efficiency of the traditional fielder's glove. He was right.

Nevertheless, pure cultural inertia provokes baseball coaches, and fathers, and authors, forty years later to waste time and frustration trying to teach children to catch a ball between the heels of their hands. Teach your child to "trap" the ball between his fore-finger and thumb.

You will find that they will often use the opposite hand when it is helpful, but behind the glove for more squeezing ability. You can encourage this by doing it yourself instead of telling them to do something that you yourself will not do.

FLY BALLS AND POP-UPS:

There's nothing magic here. The only difference is that the youngsters have to learn to JUDGE PARABOLAS. The glove should be above the shoulders WITH THE WRIST FLOPPED BACK TO ADDRESS THE BALL PERPENDICULARLY JUST LIKE YOU PRACTICED IN THE MIRROR DRILL. Teach the children, and remind them often, to move **under** the ball so that the glove is positioned well forward of their body, above their shoulders, and that the fingers of the glove point UP

rather than side ways if they **can** position themselves **under** that ball.

Start with low arcs when they are learning, and start by simply throwing the ball. Using a soft rubber baseball look alike during the first year or two will help the children build confidence without smashed faces. (Smashes in the face tend to prolong the confidence building process, especially if a child has more imagination than the average rutabaga.)

As their confidence grows, you must continually encourage them to "move up under the ball", instead of stopping short and trying to catch it in their "skillet". "Cue": "Keep your glove **UP!** (stationary above their shoulder), **ONLY MOVE YOUR FEET TO CATCH THE BALL!**"

As time goes by, the kids will need to have balls HIT to them off a bat to help them learn to react toward the catch point quickly. For the first year or two, thrown balls will suffice.

NOTE ONE: The idea is to run as fast as possible to the expected catch point, and then stop and wait for the ball.

NOTE TWO: A lot of times that's not possible, so the kids need to learn to run without their heels touching the ground. That way the ball doesn't seem to be bouncing around in their vision from the jarring of their heels impacting the ground as they run. I get my kids to hustle better going on and off the field by making a drill of running on their toes. "O.K. guys, EVERYBODY FLOAT!" As sure as the world, you're going to get some wisecracks and that just makes it more fun and more memorable.

GROUND BALLS:

There is a popular book about how to play baseball out there that shows your kids how to lay their glove down like a "dust pan", and is the FASTEST WAY I KNOW TO GET YOUR CHILD A SMASHED FACE AND A PERMANENT FLINCH! If they have played any ball, they probably already have a flinch from having a ball climb their glove and arm at some time or other. It's a pretty memorable experience!

You will need to work hard to break the bad habits with the catching method we have been teaching all along. The glove is positioned facing the ball perpendicularly, the arms close together protect your kid's belly, and you can still hope to be a grandfather.

Finally, by having the glove ALMOST <u>VERTICALLY</u> POSITIONED BACK, JUST IN FRONT OF THEIR TOES, A RICOCHET OFF THEIR GLOVE OR ARMS WILL BE DIRECTED OUT IN FRONT OF THEM, instead of up into their face.

As they **dip down** to field the ball, their arms will be pointing straight down, just forward enough to allow them to swing them side to side in front of their knees.

This is the ground-ball technique made famous by "The Wizard", Ozzie Smith, Shortstop for the St. Louis Cardinals. As Art Howe put it: "Of course Ozzie does it better than anyone! He's a magnificent athlete to start with, but he is also showing three times more glove to the ball than anyone else. He looks like he's addressing a ball with a bushel basket!"

Not only will the kids avoid being hurt; they can still pick the ball up and get a lot of runners out! If the ball has been hit so softly that they can safely "dust-pan" it, they probably ought to bare-hand it instead...and WHEN YOU BARE-HAND IT, PICK IT UP <u>BESIDE</u> YOU SO YOU DON'T KICK IT.

Next we need to talk about having the kids learn to "PLAY THE HOPS". The easiest method to teach them how to catch grounders is to instruct them, and endlessly remind them, THAT THEY CHARGE EVERY SINGLE GROUND BALL!

If you can get them to charge consistently, all kinds of neat things start to happen. Perhaps <u>most</u> important, the "charge" activates, **triggers**, their entire set of reflex mechanisms. Instead of being reduced to a passive receiver, and having to take whatever a batter dishes out, they are moving and acting...and **<u>choosing</u>** how to get a glove on that ball.

If a given ball is hit too hard for them to charge, their very preparedness to charge will trigger those reflexes, **and still allow them to make the best of a difficult situation**. They will have rocked forward onto their toes, moving on the ball.

What we are striving to teach here is to <u>catch the ball on the way down off the hop,</u> <u>or just an instant after it leaves the ground</u>. You can explain it to the kids by showing them that those are the only two places that are predictable. If they can charge enough to intercept the ball at one of those points, things get enormously easier.

If the ball isn't hopping at all, but is a <u>skinner</u> instead, that's fine too. Interestingly enough if the spin on a <u>skinner</u> induces a late hop, holding the glove and body the way we've demonstrated, (glove low, rear end low), the fielder can come UP extremely fast for it. IN FACT, THEY CAN COME UP MUCH FASTER THAN THEY CAN GO DOWN. As we discussed earlier in the chapter on hitting, GRAVITY LIMITS OUR ACCELERATION DOWNWARD, BUT ADRENALINE CAN PUSH US <u>UP</u> UNBELIEVABLY FAST.

Some so-called teaching books I have read spend a lot of time discussing "the cross over step" to teach a kid how to move laterally to get in front of a ball. Yes, your fielders can move laterally quite fast that way, but they are sure going to have a tough time catching a ball running at a 90% angle to it.

I TEACH THE SHUFFLE METHOD where the kids move the foot closest to the path of the ball first and try to KEEP their legs from crossing. It makes a lot more sense because it keeps them facing the ball squarely in

order to try to catch it BETWEEN THEIR KNEES, which is what you want them to strive to do.

At extreme lateral range, they are going to "cross over" and run anyway. Wish them luck! If they manage to stab a ball, they just robbed a base hit and everybody should cheer, A LOT!

FINAL NOTE:

If you think screaming "USE BOTH HANDS" is a fun thing to do, fine. I can tell you though, "It ain't gonna' happen." Persuading your kids to use both hands to catch a ball is going to be like talking them into putting training wheels back on their bikes. One-handing a ball seems to be a mark of growing up or something. Don't worry about it. If you successfully ingrain the "forefinger-thumb" concept, they will do all right with today's modern gloves, with...

...PRACTICE, PRACTICE, PRACTICE!

**Two finger <u>pads</u> on seam
(Not finger tips)**

Thumb on slick white part

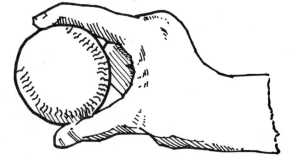

Space between ball and web

CHAPTER FOUR

THROWING A BALL
(Pitching Later)

This subject is by far the most difficult to discuss with the written word and <u>still</u> pictures. Throwing a ball is by its very nature a totally fluid process, and for all practical purposes defies static description. We have to describe it nevertheless, and you will need to work at it a lot to achieve that fluidity.

◄ THE GRIP

The PADS of the fore-finger and the second finger must **ALWAYS** be **ACROSS** a seam, **NEVER ALONG THE SEAMS**. For youngsters with their smaller fingers, placing their fingers **along the seams** spreads their fingers too far apart and costs them a lot of velocity, with no appreciable increase in accuracy.

Spreading their two fingers **one of <u>their</u> finger-widths** apart offers the best compromise between accuracy and velocity. Their other two fingers should be curled up, creating a cradle for the ball.

Their thumb should be exactly opposite their fingers on a slick white part of the ball to allow back spin for longer flatter throws.

The back-spin on that ball is very important because the ball will try to climb, in spite of gravity, because of both the aerodynamics **and** the gyro effect of that spin. Leave a gap between the ball and the web formed between their fingers and thumb, again to allow that back-spin and to increase velocity and range for a given amount of effort.

DRILL POSITION: INTRODUCTORY

Have your youngsters turn <u>**sideways**</u> to you with their throwing arm almost fully extended TO THE SIDE. Their feet **must** be turned sideways to you also. The ball will be on the side <u>away</u> from you, glove side <u>toward</u> you.

Have them lean sideways from the hips away from you, then tell them to "COME <u>HIGH</u> OVER THE TOP AND LET HER RIP!"

As they do so, they should be pushing off their "throwing foot", (defined as the same side foot as their "throwing arm").

They must be stepping directly toward you with their "catching foot", and that foot **must** come down with the toe pointed straight at you.

Their "throwing foot" should be dragging behind their follow through to arrest the twisting momentum their shoulder and body rotation has induced.

CONGRATULATIONS DAD! You have just taught a youngster to throw correctly, not only with his arm, but using his body, shoulders, and legs as well. You have just taught him a concept that a lot of big leaguers haven't learned yet, AND IT REALLY IS JUST THAT SIMPLE.

Don't get bogged down with a lot of the useless verbiage you will hear and read out there. You will hear all about a lot of <u>dont's</u>, but they simply constitute a vocabulary of defeat!

You, on the other hand, have set up a simple drill that with a few **million** repetitions will give your kids a smooth, consistent delivery, ever increasing in power and range.

Some kids want to "PUSH" the ball rather than throwing it, so always check to make sure your students are completing their arm motion with a strong downward "WRIST-FLICK". That "wrist-flick" should be slightly **across** their body, ALLOWING THEIR ELBOW TO MOVE <u>**OUTSIDE**</u> THEIR THROWING HAND.

(If your youngsters have a problem getting that elbow "**out**", simply get them to drop down and throw a little more "three-quarters".)

One interesting observation I've made is that children always seem to pick up on exactly the things we wish they wouldn't. When we are playing catch with our kids, especially the younger ones, we tend to delete any shoulder rotation on our part to keep from throwing too hard to them. They will mimic us just as sure as the world in this unless we make the point over and over again not to.

Girls especially have a difficult time getting their shoulder rotation going, and it's probably due to unconsciously copying their throwing partners. The drill outlined above **will** conquer those bad tendencies, for boys and girls alike.

THE HOP AND SKIP

All this means is to do the stepping as described above, TWICE! I'm being slightly facetious here, but only slightly. For longer, more powerful throws, sort of hopping the first step onto the "catching foot", (and without crossing their legs with the so-called "crow hop"), then "skipping" and pushing and throwing on the second step, is all they need to learn...ever! As they get older and stronger they will revert to the single push more and more often.

Left handers ALWAYS look strange throwing a ball. In fact, SOUTHPAWS always throw "three quarters". (That means a little side-arm.) I asked a doctor about it once and he muttered something to the effect that: "Of course you do my boy. Your heart is closer to your left arm. Your perfleiz-iclelch arteries don't have as much room to flex and stretch and your muzermunepolis is shaped differently..." He went on like that for some time but you probably have the picture.

What you and your students are trying to achieve is a flowing, powerful motion, and a good way to help them is to let them throw to someone else while you watch from their back-side to see if you can detect any wrinkles or unnecesary hitches or joint-snaps. Don't let them try to "aim" the ball. A smooth motion as described above and concentration on their target will gradually come together into what is called hand-eye coordination.

A fun way to transfer the idea to the kids is to ask them if they can place their fore-finger in their left nostril without aiming. Get them to try it. Yecchh! "O K, if you can do that, you can throw a ball without aiming too."

GREAT DRILLS

Get your kids to drop the ball on the ground after catching it. Then have them scoop it up in their glove, very very quickly, and (CUE), "**SLAP TWO FINGERS ACROSS A SEAM, right there in the glove! Grip it and fire it!**"

After they get comfortable with that, (twenty repititions?), then tell them: "**OK, now find the proper grip without looking at the ball.**"

If you can get them to grip the ball correctly enough times, they won't revert and **palm it** when the pressure is on. Pretty soon their fingers will find the grip automatically. This is especially helpful early each season.

Start each throwing session with the kids ten steps from you, (30 feet), and have them throw gently, but correctly as described above. After fifteen tosses or so, have them step back another five paces, (45 feet), and complete their warming up.

Now step back another fifteen steps, (a total distance of around 90 feet), and continue for another fifteen or twenty throws. When you establish this distance, **begin**

throwing to a point on the ground fifteen feet or so in front of each other and catch the ball on the long bounce.

This is a great drill to instill confidence in both throwers and receivers. It also reinforces the idea that a flat throw is better than one of those worthless, high looping "MOCKING BIRD-KILLERS". As you will see, this will be very important when we start infield and outfield practice. (P.S. The long hop is easier to catch than a short hop.)

Another drill that helps the youngsters get full arm extension into their throws and reminds them to throw overhand: get them to kneel down and throw, about ten steps from each other. I'm not sure exactly why it works, but it does.

A highschool coach that reviewed this book suggested the reason is that the kids MUST use full extension and the **"WRIST-FLICK"** to keep from falling on their faces. Show them how to twist their upper bodies to mimic the sideways stance AND SHOULDER ROTATION described above.

The **"FLIP-IT DRILL"** is very important to spend some time on because there are a lot of occasions when your players need a **QUICK AND VISIBLE** short throw technique.

They need the quick release in order to get a runner out, and they need a visible starting point so the throw's receiver can focus on the ball early enough to catch it at short range.

Have the kids pair off six long steps from each other, (15 to 18 feet), hold their throwing hand with the ball **high**

above their head, and **"flip"** the ball from there. They use only their forearm and wrist for the "flip", they want to flip the ball chest-high to their partner, and you want to have them begin flipping harder and harder as their confidence grows.

(Final variation on the drill): Have the "flipper" run forward five or six steps before "flipping", as their partner backpeddles rapidly, to receive the flip. Then they quickly switch roles and both run the other direction. This is a terrific way to teach the skills involved in a rundown situation.

With these drills, we have given the kids all the basics they need. The remaining throwing skills they will need to master must be practiced live in situations play, but incorporating these basics.

HAVE FUN!

Playing The Outfield

A lot of kids think the outfield is Siberia to which they are exiled because they aren't good enough to play the infield. I must also admit that many Managers don't know any better than to act as if that were the case. Let's talk about some of the things a motivated outfielder can do to WIN GAMES.

First, impress upon your outfielders that each base advanced by a runner is 1/4th of a run. In each game they play, count the number of 1/4ths they save by being a hustler and a "BACKER-UPPER"! You and your outfielders will both be surprised at how often THEY make the difference in winning and losing.

Second, I suppose it's painfully obvious, but I have to say it anyway lest we forget. **Their _primary_ job is to catch, block, fall on, stomp, shoot, bite, kick, and question the ancestry of every ball hit into their ARC-OF RESPONSIBILITY; TO-KEEP-IT-IN-FRONT-OF-THEM!** By simply accomplishing that, they have saved at least 2/4ths of a run, and probably 4/4ths.

If they catch a ball in the air, they have saved 4/4ths of a run, plus another 4/4ths for every runner on base when the catch is made. If they fire it to the correct base, INSTANTLY, they have saved another 1/4th of a run.

Wow, during the course of a game those /4ths add up in a hurry!

Stop the ball somehow!

POSITIONING:

I often position my outfielders quite a lot closer to the infield than do most managers. They are going to get a ball hit over their heads occasionally, but in the mean time, they are catching those looping Texas leaguers and deep pop-ups for outs. In addition, they are in a better position to play their back-up role.

I position them IN THE GAPS about 20 feet behind the closest infielders when the oldest kids are nine years old, 35 feet behind the infielders for ten and eleven year olds and perhaps 40 feet deep through age twelve, EXCEPT AGAINST THE STRONGEST HITTERS AND IN SIT-UATIONS WHEN A BALL HIT BEYOND THEM WILL LOSE THE GAME.

The right fielders on my teams are a special case. Unless they are facing a left-handed hitter, I usually position them **just** **two steps onto the outfield grass, half way between first and second base.** (I also cheat my second baseman over to within ten feet of second base as we will discuss in the chapter on infield play.)

My right fielders are now in an excellent position to catch those "pooch" flys so often hit to the opposite field, and they make great EXTRA INFIELDERS. On a ground ball, they are taught to charge hard and make the play at first or second, just like a second baseman would.

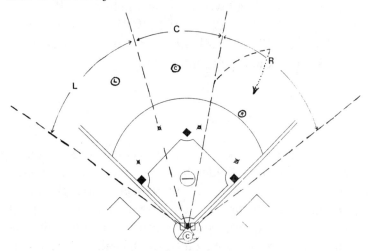

ARCS OF RESPONSIBILITY

If a ball is hit out of our outfielders' "ARC OF RESPON-SIBILITY", THEIR ROLE CHANGES TO "SAFETY MAN"! If the ball is hit to their neighboring outfielder, they should be running toward the back-up position to that neighbor, screaming at the top of their lungs, over and over again, where to throw the ball. Again, if the ball is hit out of their "ARC OF RESPONSIBILITY", but to the infield, or the opposite field, they should be moving to their back-up position at <u>THEIR BASE</u>.

In the questionable zones along the interfaces between the arcs of responsibility, most coaches give the right-of-way to the center fielder. The right and left fielders defer to the center fielder in all cases. If there is a collision between outfielders, it is never the center fielder's fault, but the knot on his head won't feel any better for all that. It is **THE CENTER FIELDERS' JOB** to call for the ball and call off their fellow outfielder. Don't let them be timid about it.

The left fielder backs up 3rd, the center fielder backs up 2nd, and the right fielder backs up 1st, and all back-ups should ideally be made 20 to 30 feet behind the person they are backing-up. At that distance they have time to react to a ball that gets by the primary receiver they are backing-up. Score your outfielders 1/4th of a run every time they remember to back up **their base**.

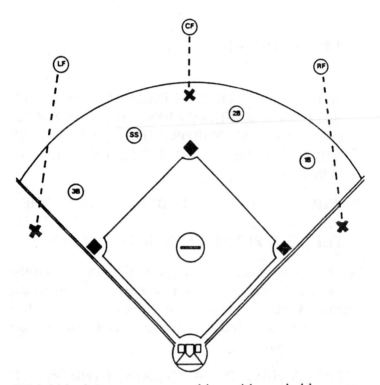

With kids the age we are working with, probably a quarter of the throws around the infield go astray. Since so many outfielders are improperly coached, or uncoached, or ignored until after the key play is over, YOUR outfielder is going to be an unwelcome surprise to A BUNCH of base runners.

They are going to throw a lot of runners out too, because if they field the over-throw cleanly, you are going to encourage them to complete the play, **"and nail that sucker!"**...

...in which case you will score them 4/4ths of a run, and you are going to have a proud and happy kid on your hands...and you will want to buy them an ice cream cone on the way home after the game!

RULES OF THUMB:

1. WHEN YOUR OUTFIELDERS CATCH A FLY BALL, OR SOMEHOW KEEP A BALL IN FRONT OF THEM, THEY THROW THE BALL <u>ONE BASE</u> AHEAD OF THE <u>LEAD</u> RUNNER'S STARTING POSITION.

2. WHEN THE BALL GETS BEHIND THEM, THEY THROW THE BALL <u>TWO BASES</u> AHEAD OF THE LEAD RUNNER'S STARTING POSITION.

You can even insert the word <u>ALWAYS</u> and not go too far wrong. Its better for them to have a SIMPLE, but DEFINITE plan in mind before a given play, rather than to be indecisive. Indecision causes bad throws, late throws, and runs scored.

ALL THEY HAVE TO CALCULATE IS THE ONE OR TWO BASES AHEAD OF THAT LEAD RUNNER'S STARTING POSITION.

(Example: "If I catch it, throw to 2nd. If it gets past me, throw to 3rd." This is an example only. Now <u>you</u> tell me where I have placed the lead runner to make this example. Simple, huh?)

3. NOBODY ON BASE? THROW IT TO 2ND BASE!

4. Hopefully, there is a cut-off-man with both hands extended over his head. Regardless, teach your outfielder to throw the ball toward the correct base with a low trajectory, flat, so an alert cut-off-man can make a variation play if necessary. The Cue: "NO MOCK-ING-BIRD-KILLERS, GUYS."

5. If they are going to have to make a critical throw, teach them to be moving toward the infield as they make their catch. That way they can begin their hop-and-skip, (without crossing their legs or ankles), quickly, and get that extra momentum into their throw.

CONCLUSIONS:

ON MOST BALL CLUBS, THE OUTFIELDERS ARE NOT UTILIZED VERY WELL, COACHED VERY WELL, OR SHOWN ENOUGH RESPECT. The result is that a full 1/3rd of the team's defensive assets are wasted. A respected, well coached outfield WILL make the difference in EVERY game.

EVERY OUTFIELDER SHOULD BE MOVING ON EVERY PLAY, AND EVERY OUTFIELDER IS IN ON EVERY PLAY.

**"Ready Position: Knees Bent,
Throwing Hand In The Glove!"**

Playing The Infield

Position your infielders fairly deep except when there might be a critical play at the plate. Ten feet behind the imaginary baselines for 1st, 2nd, and 3rd basemen, and fifteen or even twenty feet for your shortstop. They are, after all, well-trained and conditioned to charge every single ball hard aren't they? Of course!

They are also in their **"ready positions"** to catch the hard smash, or at least knock it down, in order to throw the force out.

MINDSET is especially important for infielders. They have to **know** where they are going to throw the ball if it's softly hit, or if it is hit sharply.

(HIT SHARPLY? FORCE THE LEAD RUNNER. HIT SOFTLY? GO TO FIRST.) If they fumble a little they are going to have to go for first, or even hold the ball if it's more than a momentary fumble. In fact, sometimes, holding the ball and checking the situation is the best play if they don't field the ball cleanly.

If the ball is NOT hit into a particular infielder's arc of responsibility, he should be <u>SPRINTING</u> toward the base he is responsible for helping cover. He might be seriously needed there in a minute.

CUT-OFFS AND RELAYS:

Each manager has his own preferences on who-cuts-off-where. Get your infielder to pay attention, and ask questions if he isn't sure. A couple of principles <u>ARE</u> always valid though.

1. ON RELAY/CUT-OFFS, the **relay/cut-off-man** lines up <u>EXACTLY</u> with the base where the play is going to be made, BOTH HANDS EXTENDED ABOVE HIS HEAD.

2. If the throw is coming true toward the base, and the out can still be made there, HE LETS THE BALL GO THROUGH AND GETS OUT OF THE WAY. He only cuts it off if the ball is out of steam and rolling, going wide of the base, or if the runner has already beaten the play. If THE RUNNER has already beaten the play, and he sees another runner he thinks he can get out, he cuts the ball off and makes his throw. Hard! Its aways a tough decision, based purely on judgment. Wish him the best of luck!

RUNDOWNS:

There are TWO objectives when running a base runner down.

1. Obviously the most hoped for outcome is to get the runner out.

2. What might NOT be so obvious is that running them back to the base they started from is ALMOST AS GOOD!

Try to make the TAG while the runner is trying to get back to that starting point. If your infielders can catch the runner without throwing at all, they are miles ahead.

As the kids get older, they will learn extremely sophisticated run-down drills such as the "circle-drill" and/or the "criss-cross-drill". At this level of play, **teach them to keep their throws to an absolute minimum**.

In any case, they always push the runner as far as possible toward his starting point consistent with a "FLIP AND CATCH" to put him out.

The infielders always run with the ball above their head IN CLEAR VIEW OF THEIR PARTNER, any time they are in a run-down situation.

Your infielders should always run <u>HARD</u> and make the runner commit toward his starting point. Then they FLIP HIM OUT. If he is the partner on the end of the rundown closest to the runner's starting point, you want HIM to <u>CHARGE HARD TOO</u>, but not for very far. As soon as the runner commits toward the advanced base, HE FLIPS the ball to his partner ahead of the runner, UNLESS HE IS POSITIVELY, ABSOLUTELY, (PRETTY SURE), HE CAN CATCH THAT RUNNER!

COACHING HINTS TO FIRST BASEMEN

1. Don't charge bunts! Let the pitcher or catcher field them because I'll guarantee you someone will forget to cover your abandoned base.

2. A HUGE STRETCH is impressive to look at, but it won't make a difference in one out of twenty plays. In youth leagues you will get a LOT higher percentage of bad throws than one in twenty. Instead, stand square to the throw in a fielding ready position, knees considerably bent, (but both hands high over your head), with your <u>THROWING FOOT ON TOP OF THE BAG WITH YOUR TOE EVEN WITH THE EDGE OF THAT BAG TOWARD THE INFIELD!</u> That way when you step forward to make the catch, your toe is still in good contact with the bag.

If the throw is nearly perfect, then you can step toward it with your CATCHING foot to receive it in a moderate stretch.

3. Your first priority is to CATCH THE BALL AT ALL COSTS. Only then worry about fishing around for the bag you left while CATCHING THE BALL!!!

HINTS TO SECOND BASEMEN

1. Try to remember to cover first base if the first baseman is off doing something stupid, like fielding a bunt!

2. ALWAYS straddle the base when you are going to have to TAG a runner out upon receiving a throw from your catcher. Very seldom will you ever have to TAG a runner out unless he is stealing, in which case you will be facing first base with your tender li'l feet safely out of the way. One foot will be on the 3rd base side of the bag and the other will be on the right field side of the bag.

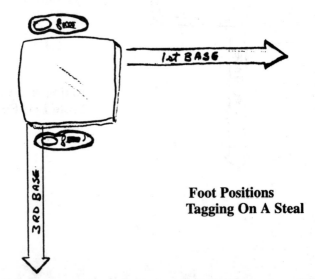

Foot Positions
Tagging On A Steal

EXCEPTIONS: Every now and then some **"knothead"** who doesn't know how efficient your outfielders are will try to stretch a single into a double. The only advice I can give you that you will remember in such an event is, <u>DON'T TURN YOUR BACK ON THE SUCKER, STANDING IN BASE-PATH, WHILE RECEIVING THE THROW!</u> If you do, he will likely launch you into left field. Stand on the opposite side of the bag from the runner, or beside the bag, unless you are practicing to be an astronaut.

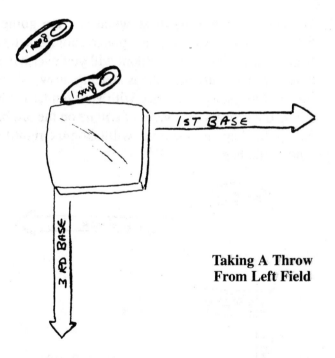

**Taking A Throw
From Left Field**

3. SLAM THE TAG DOWN SIX INCHES FROM THE BAG. Even the blindest umpire can notice when the base runner screams that you smashed his foot on a close play. He can probably also see your glove being pushed along the ground by the base runner's foot toward the bag. No guarantees here though. Some umpires are REALLY blind.

4. SLAM THE TAG DOWN WITH THE BACK OF YOUR GLOVE ON THE DIRT. That way if the runner hits or kicks your glove, the ball most likely will be squashed even more tightly into the pocket. I recommend a one-handed tag for all of you except the catcher. Its much much faster.

Making The Tag

5. On a force play, when you dont have to tag the runner, either step across the bag, stepping on it as you do, or field the throw on the side of the bag BESIDE the runner's approach. Some runners will try to slide in such a way so as to screw you into the ground or launch you into orbit. That's why they they call it "hardball". Once you make the force with your foot, BAIL OUT! and get away from the launch pad.

HINTS TO THIRD BASEMEN:

1. PLAYING A BUNT: If there's a base runner on 2nd don't charge the bunt at all! Your job is to take the throw and put him out. In fact, among guys twelve and under, I don't have my third baseman charge bunts at all. The pitcher and catcher do a pretty good job, and very few bunts roll far enough for the third baseman to worry about.

2. Third basemen have got to have a lot of courage, and a good arm. Courage because you are going to get some smashes right down your throat, and if you don't at least knock them down or block them, its almost a certain double. Those smashes also make it possible to get a lead runner at second if you field them cleanly. You've got to FIRE the ball though, whether you are going to second or going with the long throw to first.

3. FIELDING A THROW: You only have to remember ONE position except when taking a throw from your

catcher. STRADDLE THE BAG FACING SECOND BASE, WITH ONE FOOT ON THE LEFT FIELD SIDE AND ONE FOOT ON THE SIDE FACING HOME PLATE. BE TOUGH! YOU ARE THE LAST STOP BEFORE PAY DIRT. If a runner is coming toward you ahead of the ball, hold both hands up as if receiving a throw anyway. Be a good enough actor and you might get the runner to slide and waste time before turning for home. You may have just saved a run. If you are taking a throw from home plate, then just straddle the bag facing home.

4. Position yourself ten to fifteen feet behind the imaginary line from second to third when getting ready to field hit balls, about ten feet toward second base from the foul line. YOU HAVE TO CHARGE ESPECIALLY HARD ON SOFTLY HIT BALLS BECAUSE OF THE LONG THROW YOU HAVE TO MAKE, BUT PLAY DEEP ANYWAY AND YOU WILL STOP A LOT OF TWO BASE HITS AND EVEN AN OCCASIONAL TRIPLE.

HINTS TO A SHORTSTOP

1. You will want to play at least fifteen feet behind the imaginary line from second base to third base. You will want to cheat over toward second from the halfway point because so many little leaguers hit through the middle.

2. You will have to charge awfully fast on softly hit balls because you are playing so deep and are going to have such a long throw to first.

3. On left-handed hitters you will be protecting second base from a steal, or when a ball is hit to right field. (See the hints to second basemen on covering the bag.)

4. You need to practice a sort of under-handed or side arm FLIP to second base, A LOT, to make the put-out on a lead runner heading for second. You are really going to need that quick release.

5. Your manager will assign you some of the most challenging cut-off and relay plays, and he will be counting on you to do a lot of other chores that some of the other kids just aren't up to. Try to be worthy of his trust.

THE CHALLENGE

Dad, an ongoing problem in virtually every organized baseball league I've been associated with is that of nepotism, and/or favoritism. Even the most fair-minded managers and coaches have inadvertantly fallen into this trap, and usually in spite of the best of motives.

The **only** sure method I've found to correct the problem is by introducing a **"mandatory challenge"** schedule into the team's practice routine. Insisting on this as a way of injecting some objectivity into position assignments and playing time decisions is your best hedge against having your child consigned to a season-long wasteland. If he works hard, he can hope to win a position, or a starting assignment, as soon as he's earned it. Conversely, he must work hard to **maintain** his position or starting assignment.

First, develop **and implement** a "challenge" test for a given position with some clearly observable scoring criteria such as catching, throwing, and situational thinking.

Second, accept the idea that the only fair way to base position decisions is upon the child's potential contribution to the team effort judged on those criteria.

Finally, insist on at least a bi-weekly schedule of challenges, (but only for one position each time, please).

The Batteries

(Pitcher and Catcher)

A lot of would-be teachers and coaches separate catching and pitching into two different categories. I was a pitcher and I can tell you from experience: THAT IS POOR JUDGEMENT.

Ask your pitchers and catchers just why these two are <u>called</u> the batteries! Right! Because the machine can't run without them: ie. "WELL O.K. GUYS, HOW WELL CAN A MACHINE RUN WITH ONE BATTERY DEAD? WORSE, HOW WELL COULD IT RUN IF THE BATTERIES WERE HOOKED UP CROSS WIRED AND OPPOSING EACH OTHER?"

The catcher can make or break any pitcher. He can break him with no one the wiser, and he can make him with very few observant enough to see it. You managers out there need to figure out how to help these guys be good friends, and you can start by NOT putting them in opposition to each other.

Here are some concepts, mind-sets, and sermon-ettes you will find yourself needing to preach to your pitchers and catchers from time to time.

PITCHER, you had better get off your high horse and start appreciating your catcher, and thanking him for helping make you successful.

Have you happened to notice, in the big leagues the manager more often than not consults his catcher before replacing a pitcher. In those conferences on the mound those managers are asking the catcher: "Does he have his "stuff" tonight? Have you seen what he is doing wrong?"

When that catcher tells his manager: "He's right around the strike zone, boss. I believe we should give him a chance to find his groove. He's hot!" the manager usually nods his head and walks back to the dugout.

The reason he does that is he **knows** his catcher has a more intimate knowledge, feel if you will, for where the pitcher's head is, than anyone around that field.

CATCHER, you owe it to your team mates to get the best out of your pitcher that he has to give. You do that by encouraging him <u>all the time</u>. If he is a jerk, I'm sorry. Pitchers sometimes are. The pressure gets so intense sometimes that he ignores everyone else.

Sometimes he couldn't hit the strike zone if it were strapped to his bottom. When you realize that, call time out and go talk to him. He can't just quit. He has to get somebody to notice that his reflexes flew north for some reason and get him out of there. He doesn't want to let you guys down. Really and truly.

PITCHER, when you get on the pitching rubber, you and your catcher ought to be reading each other's minds. PAY ATTENTION to what your catcher is showing you. He is telling you stuff all the time. You don't need to worry about the score, or the fielders, or the runners, or anything except what your catcher is telling you.

CATCHER, if you are the shy, quiet type, GET OVER IT! YOU ARE THE FIELD GENERAL, SO START LIVING UP TO YOUR RESPONSIBILITY! Your pitcher has enough on his mind trying to throw strikes, and you are the only player on the field who can see EVERYONE from the batter's perspective. You can tell if your outfielders are properly positioned in the gaps between the infielders, you can see if the base runners are paying attention to their coaches and maybe taking a signal, and you can see if one of your team mates is doping off. TAKE CHARGE!

That DOESN'T mean to be an arrogant goofus. Everything you tell your fielders should be positive in nature. For instance: DON'T YELL: "HEY THIRD, WAKE UP! CHASE BUTTERFLIES LATER!" Nope, you might feel like saying something like that, but say instead, "HEY RONNY, (ALWAYS CALL HIM BY

NAME), YOU CAN FORGET THAT GUY ON THIRD, WE'VE GOT TWO OUTS SO LET'S GUN DOWN THE GUY AT FIRST!"

I guarantee you "Ronny" will wake up, at least for a little while.

O.K., here are some other things you can YELL to your fielders to help keep them alert.

(Remember, ALWAYS begin with their name!)

You see the right-handed batter swinging late: "HEY JOE SECOND, HE'S HITTING TO YOU. WATCH HIM!"

You don't know if its a "steal" situation or not, but you have a left-handed batter: "ALL RIGHT FRANK SHORT-STOP, THE RUNNER AT FIRST THINKS HE CAN STEAL ON ME. YOU'VE GOT SECOND, RIGHT?"

You have runners on the bases and you aren't even sure what you should do: "HEY COACH JONES, DO WE WANT TO GET THE GUY AT FIRST OR DO WE NEED THE LEAD RUNNER? ...O.K. GUYS, LET'S GET HIM AT THIRD IF WE CAN! O.K.?"

I hope you are getting the idea by now, but sit down and write up a list of good things to say to your guys, then go over the list with your dad or your coach to make sure none of them will hurt somone's feelings. Then practice saying them, OUT LOUD TO YOURSELF.

P.S. Always lift off your mask to yell stuff. The guys won't be able to hear you very well with it on.

PITCHER, let your catcher be field General. Your job is to hit his target and either strike batters out or make them hit dribblers and pop ups.

CATCHER, Your job here is to give your pitcher a **GOOD** TARGET! What is a good target?

A. Your target is placed **KNEE-HIGH TO THE BATTER and CENTERED ON YOUR BODY MASS**.

B. Your target **and body** are offset **six inches off the center-line of the plate, ON EVERY PITCH**.

C. "Wink" the pocket of your mitt at your pitcher, just as he looks up to throw. That **quick little** movement will attract his eye and help his hand to follow.

D. Work the strong batters, (the top five in the batting order), on the **outside corner** and the weaker batters on the **inside corner**.

If your pitcher keeps missing the strike zone off the <u>outside</u> corner, and walking batters, you want to show him the <u>inside</u> target for a while. YOU CAN OFTEN GET HIM TO THROW HIS PITCHES INTO THE STRIKE ZONE JUST BY HELPING LIKE THAT.

PITCHER, Don't ever **THINK** outside or inside! Just throw to the target. More often than not your eye and hand will cooperate. Its your catcher's job to THINK! Your job is to relax and let your body RESPOND!

CATCHER, when I tell you to show a target on the corners, I DON'T mean on the EXACT corners of the plate, but just **four to six** inches or so off of center. Do this any time a pitcher is warming up to you while you are in a catcher's crouch. Certainly do it at all times in a game unless the pitcher is having trouble throwing strikes at all. Then try the corner that can help him best like we talked about.

PITCHER, when you throw a wild pitch and it gets by your catcher and rolls to the backstop, ALWAYS MOVE TOWARD HOME PLATE TO TAKE THE THROW BACK FROM YOUR CATCHER! You ought to tell him, "SORRY", but even more important, you should PROVE you are sympathetic for him having to run back to the backstop to retreive the wild pitch. By walking, OR RUNNING TO THE PLATE IF THERE IS A PLAYER ON BASE, you are saving your catcher HALF of the work of retreiving YOUR wild pitch.

Now he must only sprint TO THE BACKSTOP. If you don't meet him at the plate, he has to run the ball BACK IN, <u>TOO!</u> If you are standing right in front of the plate, he can THROW the ball back in and walk back to his position while you walk to the mound with the ball. If there are RUNNERS on base, you will want to keep them honest by checking on them as soon as your catcher throws you the ball.

CATCHER, if your pitcher forgot to come to the plate, YOU MUST RUN THE BALL IN BEFORE YOU THROW IT ANYWHERE. DON'T THROW A BALL ANYWHERE FROM THE BACKSTOP <u>EXCEPT TO THE PLATE!</u>

PITCHER, if your catcher misses the ball and it is rolling around on the ground, point at it and yell "THERE IT IS! THERE IT IS!" If there are runners on base, RUN TOWARD HIM YELLING AND <u>POINTING!</u> You two guys can get a lot of people out IF YOU ARE WORK-ING TOGETHER.

O.K. guys, let's talk about fielding.

PITCHER, any time a ball is hit to the first base side of the infield, anywhere on your left, move quickly toward first base without even thinking about it until you are moving. There are all sorts of ways you can help out over there. Once you are moving that direction, then start fig-uring out how you can help out. You might be required to cover first base, or perhaps back up the first baseman. You might have to change direction and move to home. Whatever the case, **get moving toward first base and then start figuring it out.**

CATCHER, guys your age don't usually bunt very far. You are the best player to field a bunt because you are facing the runners, so if you can get to a bunt, YELL OFF your team mates. YELL, "I'VE GOT IT! I'VE GOT IT!"......LOUDLY! And of course you have snatched off your mask, haven't you?

PITCHER, you need to always end your pitch delivery in the fielding position because in a fraction of a second, BAM! you are either an infielder or you're dead meat!

EVERY TIME YOU ARE PRACTICING PITCHING, practice tucking your glove up next to your catching shoulder. Yes, the back of your glove will be facing the hit ball. That's O.K.! You can slap that ball away from your face in an instant if it is a line smash, and you can move your glove to catch a grounder fast enough to catch moderately hit balls. Don't be waving your glove around in the breeze somewhere. TUCK IT IN!

CATCHER, If your pitcher is continually throwing high, he's not following through good enough. Yell, "COME ON DOWN THE MOUND TO ME, JIM-BOB PITCHER."

PITCHER, if your catcher yells that to you it will help if you finish your delivery with a couple of "chop-chop" steps toward him, hunkered over like an infielder.

CATCHER, You are going to get dirtier, tireder, sweatier, and more generally bunged up than anyone on the team. If you can't handle it, **Don't Be A Catcher!**

Don't be caught holding your throwing hand behind you like a SISSY either! Don't argue with anyone about it, just "forget" accidently. They are only trying to keep you from getting hurt, and somewhere along the line they heard it was a good idea to help keep you from getting your throwing hand hit by a foul tip. (JUST BETWEEN YOU AND ME, YOU PUT THAT THROWING HAND DIRECTLY BEHIND YOUR MITT **IN A LOOSE FIST!**)

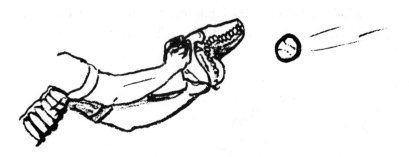

Making it a **loose fist, thumb curled,** will keep anything from being broken, even if you do get it hit once or twice in your lifetime. Those guys sticking their hand behind them are going to be hit on the funny bone instead, AND

THAT AIN'T FUNNY. Who knows, you might decide to be a hero some day when the game depends on it, and reach out with that bare hand and knock down a wild pitch. Hands heal, but lost championships don't!

PITCHER, while we are talking about courage here, when you throw a wild pitch with a man on third in a close game, YOU CHARGE HOME, AND AS YOU RECEIVE THE THROW FROM YOUR CATCHER AT THE BACKSTOP, TURN YOUR LEGS TOWARD THIRD BASE WITH YOUR KNEES BENT, LEFT FOOT <u>TOUCHING</u> THE BASELINE A STEP TOWARD THIRD FROM THE PLATE, AND TAKE THE SLIDE, HOPEFULLY, JUST TO YOUR LEFT.

This is a lesson on playing "REAL" baseball so I don't have to admit you MIGHT get "clobbered" doing this, but I will tell you anyway. **YOU MIGHT GET CLOBBERED DOING THIS,** but the question is whether that particular run is worth getting clobbered for.

CATCHER, You are wearing shin guards, a chest protector, and a cup. Your job is to block the runner from getting to home plate AT ALL COSTS. When taking a throw from one of your team mates in the field its a pretty good idea to pretty well face the thrower in the fielding position so you can at least try to block a poor throw. You should be positioned ONE LONG STEP TOWARD THIRD, WITH KNEES BENT, JUST BARELY ON THE FAIR SIDE OF THE FOUL LINE.

As a pretty good throw approaches, turn to your left and PLACE YOUR LEFT FOOT **ON** THE FOUL LINE, KNEES BENT.

A good coach I know says it quite humorously: "Ya' gotta give the runner the back corner of the plate to slide to until ya' got the ball! YOU'VE GIVETH...NOW TAKETH IT AWAY!"

Keeping your head up so you can see the runner, prepare for the impact as you are receiving the throw. One good way to prepare for that impact is to cup your throwing hand over the ball in your mitt so when the runner blasts you out of your shin guards, you don't drop the ball.

FACING the oncoming runner with your knees bent will prevent you from getting a knee knocked out. Knees are quite strong from the front, but very vulnerable from the side.

LEARN TO GET THAT FACE MASK OFF ANY TIME
THERE IS A PLAY GOING ON SO YOU CAN SEE
BETTER.

PITCHER AND CATCHER, for well over a hundred
years a put-out at the plate has been the most exciting
play in baseball. If you DO get clobbered, I hope it makes
you feel better to know that every old grey-headed former pitcher and catcher who ever played the game smiles
deep down inside for you, and is proud that America
STILL produces youngsters with courage, fortitude, and
the willingness to "TAKE ONE ON THE NOGGIN FOR
THEIR TEAM MATES."

Running The Bases
(Sliding is the Fastest Way to Stop)

We are working with kids from age seven through twelve years old here, so let's keep things in perspective. With beginners, the first drill you want to practice might simply be letting the kids follow you around the bases a few times to get in the habit of running to first base **first!**

If you are working with seven year olds for instance, you will have **six years** and a heck of a lot of fun feeding in more and more refinements as you go along. The kids will love learning more and more of the **"sneaky tricks"** you will have gleaned here, but use some judgement in the rate you do feed them in.

Most leagues involving kids twelve-years-old or less don't allow lead-offs, but if yours does, the principles I am outlining here still apply only more so.

If lead-offs **are** allowed in your league, keep your runners on **first base** or **third base** until the pitcher steps on the rubber. Then have them take **exactly THREE steps** off the base and stop. (The Cue: "THREE ARE FREE! THREE ARE FREE!") Then get them **walking** briskly toward the next base as the pitcher begins the move toward home plate. They must continue this walk **one full step beyond when the catcher receives the ball.** That way, their brain is still transmitting the signal "walk", instead of the signal "stop", thus keeping momentum in their favor for the break to the next base.

If your runners are on **second base**, your Cue is: "TAKE WHAT THEY GIVE YOU! TAKE WHAT THEY GIVE YOU!" This Cue is to remind them that when on **second base**, when the pitcher steps on the pitching rubber they are to move as quickly as they can to a point **one step further from second base than the infielder closest to that base!**

(A runner can't be picked off if there is no one to catch the pick-off throw.) Your runners on second base begin their **walk** toward third base, **from that point**, as the pitcher begins the move to the plate.
(They also have to move back toward second base if one of the infielders do...they have to be alert.)

The lead-off method seemingly carved in stone tablets and passed down from mythical times is the **"sideways skip."** It is so commonly employed that we don't even question its limitations.

In reality that "skip" creates all kinds of problems. The first is that the runners skip too far, trying to mimic the older kids and get picked off. Almost as bad, the runners get excited and skip too far...**realize they are too far**...and stop, killing their momentum.

The slow controlled movement toward the next base, **walking**, will create the **momentum**, to give them a full two, or even three step advantage at the next base.

Finally, in a **steal** situation, instead of beginning their **walk** toward the next base, they take the same lead-offs I outlined above **THEN BREAK FOR THE NEXT BASE IN A FULL SPRINT!**

Using this lead-off and "break" method doesn't alert the catcher or pitcher, **allowing the runners to break much sooner and still give themselves a full two step advantage toward the next base. THEY CAN NOW "BREAK" THE INSTANT A PITCHER "WIGGLES"!**

If it turns out that the pitcher's "wiggle" is in fact a pick-off move, even though no steal attempt is apparent, the runners at this level of play can usually get to the next base successfully anyway, or will cause the pitcher to "balk."

THE BREAK FROM THE BOX:

The first and perhaps most difficult thing to teach bat-ter/runners is how important it is to get a good break from the batter's box on the way to first. It's an awkward tran-sition at best, and combined with the overwhelming urge to see where they hit it, this failure accounts for as many outs in a given ball game as any other single cause except strike outs.

There are two methods to dramatically improve the break, and together can account for an extraordinary number of runs. First, incorporate the break into the very core of your batting practices, (see chapter on practices). Second, persuade your kids that they can peek all they want to, **after** they have made their break. What you want is for them to take those first two or three crucial strides, get their forward **momentum** up, and **then** look.

We are back to that word **"momentum"** again so let's talk about it a moment. A good mathematician could whip up a formula for exactly how important elapsed time at ZERO miles per hour really is. He could then relate that ZERO to distance traveled, or lack of it, and you and I would be amazed at the difference. I do know that one ZERO in any length of column of figures lead-ing to an eventual **average** miles per hour number can change that average A LOT, and distance traveled within an elapsed time EVEN MORE. **Any** time we can take advantage of this principle we are far, far ahead.

When teaching the run to first, don't get fancy. Any gains made by the swooping turn or other big league refinements will be marginal at best, and may very well get your kids called out by an inexperienced umpire. Just show them to run just outside the white foul-line.

Teach your runners that they **do** have one decision to make while on their way to first; turn left, or turn right. They will need to turn left if the hit goes beyond the infield, and they will need to overrun and veer right if an infielder is making a play on them. THEY NEED TO BE TAUGHT TO TURN ONE WAY OR THE OTHER EVERY TIME! This pre-programming will get them to take advantage of the free overrun.

When teaching, (or endlessly reminding), your runners to make their cut to the left toward second base, coach on the things that can make the greatest difference. You will hear endless arguments about which foot is best, measuring the last three steps to get properly positioned, or whether its best to just let the kid hit the bag and keep going.

Don't worry about it. You can mention that the left foot is best, allowing the shortest series of cross over steps, but the thing you want to spend some time on is practicing letting the kids hit the **VERTICAL** EDGE CORNER of the bag with the **bottom** of their instep, or heel, and using the bag as a kind of **BANKED TURN DEVICE** like the banked turns on a racetrack.

Practice it yourself a few times before you show THEM how to do it, and save them some sprained ankles.

THE SLIDE IS THE FASTEST WAY TO STOP!

A lot of kids, and dads, and managers, don't even know that is why sliding was invented. It is **not** inherently a strategem to avoid being tagged at all, but a tactic that allows a full speed run ALL THE WAY TO THE BASE, with a quick stop at that base to keep from over running; (those miles per hour averages again). The only alternative is beginning a deceleration several steps short of the base.

Teach your kids to slide well and you will have done them a service they will thank you for as long as they play baseball. Done correctly, its fun, it doesn't skin their knees or break ankles, and its a magnificent confidence builder. The "pop-up slide" you will see recommended in other books will "pop" bones and joints most often.

This is the WRONG way to do it!

I cannot tell you how many brave, but mis—taught youngsters I have seen tear themselves up needlessly because some well-meaning, but un-taught manager hadn't taught them a HOOK SLIDE.

Get the kids to LIE down exactly as the picture on the next page shows. Make sure they are perfectly in that position, extended foot facing UP. Now explain to them that they are going to be landing and sliding on their rumps, fannys, hineys, backsides, fat bottoms, posteriors, but ONLY on ONE CHEEK!

When the laughter and comments finally slow down, explain carefully that this manuever won't work unless they are going full speed, but IF they are going full speed they won't hurt themselves anymore.

The Hook Slide

The idea is to hook the bag or plate with the toe on the doubled up leg after a slide of about a foot.

The way the leg and ankle can flex in that direction prevents sprains and breaks, so if the kid overslides, the only result is a pivot around the bag, or baseman's foot, or any other obstacle. If he underslides just a bit, all he has to do is straighten the doubled leg a little and he's there.

Now find, (or prepare), some soft dirt and use an untethered bag. Have everyone practice these slides four or five times, and explain to them that most of the time a HOOK-SLIDE to the right, (on their right cheek), also puts them on the side of the base AWAY from the approach of the ball.

STEALING A BASE:

There are **three** kinds of steal: the all-out steal, the half steal, and the delayed steal. There, that remark is sure to start some arguments, but I assure you everything else is simply a refinement or variation on these three.

You want to help the kids to learn to "spell" steal at this point. It is: s-t-e-a-l-s-l-i-d-e!

The all-out steal is simply that. Break. Boogie. Motivate. Move it. Finish with a hook slide.

The **"half-steal"** requires more of an explanation. It starts out just exactly like an all-out steal, AND I MEAN EXACTLY THAT!

At the exact instant the catcher receives the ball, the runner must break for the next base like his life depended on it, looking straight at his proposed target base. He should run that way for ONE THIRD (1/3RD) OF THE DISTANCE, AND THEN BEGIN DE-CELERATING

AND LOOKING. (You might want to give your runners a specific number of steps here.)

If the catcher is asleep and throws the ball toward THE PITCHER, OR TO FIRST BASE, BREAK AGAIN, and finish with a hook slide. Otherwise, he begins IMMEDI-ATELY retreating toward his starting point while observ-ing where the catcher throws the ball. If the catcher throws it away, he breaks for the target base and turns it for the next.

And last, my favorite, "The good ole' delayed steal". The secret here is timing and acute observation.

The runner waits at his starting point, coiling his muscles to sprint, until the <u>EXACT INSTANT</u> he <u>KNOWS</u> the catcher is throwing the ball back to the pitcher. The lazy arm motion is the key thing to watch for, but wait for the arm to be moving forward. HE EXPLODES OUT OF HIS SHOES AND GOES! ITS AN ALL OUT STEAL!...AND FINISH WITH A HOOK SLIDE!

Its a real charge to watch the catcher try to recover. Sometimes he will throw the ball straight up in the air, and sometimes in the dirt.

Sometimes he will simply stand there with his mouth open. Sometimes he will actually get the throw to the pitcher, who will himself stand there with his mouth open. Caution your runner to keep his peeking to a mini-mum.

One defenses this strategy by having the catcher always throw sharply to the pitcher, ESPECIALLY with men on base. No one can accomplish anything with a ball float-ing lazily through the air, but its fun watching the oppos-

ing manager trying to come up with a defense during the game. This is also a good time to pull a half steal next.

This next season I'm going to be working on our invisible steal. This is no joke. I've spotted a void in the rules that may actually make it possible. I won't tell you the exact idea, but it has everything to do with "running outside the baselines to avoid a tag." Only.

...It worked great! and the kids loved playing a trick on our opponents. When your opponents' infielders are positioned too shallow, your runners simply begin their steal by walking, or leading off, at a 45 degree angle toward the outfield from the baseline. Once behind the infielders' field of vision they break and run lightly until someone starts screaming and pointing, then they sprint straight toward second base...ahead of the infielder trying to cover second base.

Another thought on **momentum:** In a league where lead offs are **not** permitted, the base runner must be touching the bag until the pitched ball crosses the plate. Fine! For several seasons now it seems I always get slow runners so I began looking for an edge, and here it is.

Instead of having my runners crouched in a sprinter's stance and poised to go, we started experimenting with a running start. I had my base runners start by standing on

the **opposite** side of the bag from where they were going to run. Their **"front"** foot was in contact with the bag, and their **"back"** foot was positioned one **full**, step **away** from the bag. (ie, on first base their **"back"** foot was positioned one full step out of bounds.)

As the pitched ball passed the half-way point on the way to the plate, they learned to launch themselves forward, over, and across the bag, but still in contact with it, and found themselves at nearly full speed as they broke contact with that bag.

It got to the point where the kids started making a joke out of it. "We don't **steal** a base, Coach. We just **borrow it until the next pitch!**"

They even took the concept a step further, and began using the technique when tagging up on a fly ball.

(I must admit that we spent some time in interesting conversations with umpires, but in each case we prevailed.)

READ YOUR OWN RULEBOOK CAREFULLY, BUT IN OUR LEAGUE THE ONLY PENALTY FOR LEAVING TOO EARLY IS TO BE SENT BACK TO THE ORIGINAL BASE. IN ADDITION, IF ON A HIT BALL THE RUNNER IS FORCED, HE DOESN'T HAVE TO GO BACK ANYWAY.

NOTE:

It's a splendid idea to have each of your players add a pair of gym shorts, or better yet, sweat pant shorts to their basic uniform ensemble. Sliding pads are better, but in some parts of the country they are awfully difficult to find. The synthetic material used for uniform pants these days will surely make a "rug burn" on your child's behind.

While we are at it, another simple piece of protective gear is a pair of jockey briefs one size too small. Every jockey strap I ever used as a kid didn't fit, and they can't furnish any protection for your boy's bottom at all. Your male catchers ought to wear a pair of jockey briefs under their supporter-cup rig.

Team Managers' Section

Practice For Success

Coach, I hope you will schedule every single practice this season with two or three **"goals"** at least verbalized to yourself on the way to the field. Better still, jot them down and look at them. If they make sense to you, I promise you can get the kids to respond with concentration and enthusiasm.

Early in the season, and hopefully your league has a two or three week pre-season, your practices will be structured around **teaching**. Only later, as the season progresses, will you want the practices to evolve into the honing and polishing process based upon the elements you have taught early on.

One key thought to launch your practice planning: Every child responds best to **individual attention**, especially from the head coach.

Structure your practices so that you are physically close to each child as you teach and coach them. This technique is ever so much more effective than yelling across the field to them. Teach quietly and encouragingly, demonstrating while you are telling.

THE FIRST PRACTICE OF THE SEASON

You will want to personally invite the kids' parents to come, and stay, for your first practice. They will get to see your coaching style and become more comfortable with what their kids go home and tell them through the course of the season. In addition, perhaps they can see how much fun it can be working with the youngsters, and will come out a lot and get involved. Not only that, they will learn from you too and will reinforce the teaching you do.

Start the practice by sitting the kids down on the grass in a semi-circle and sitting down with them. The parents will probably stand, and that's O.K. My suggestion is to begin by telling the parents and players what your hopes and plans are for the season, that you are a fanatic about hustle and fundamentals, and that they are going to play in <u>DIRECT PROPORTION TO THEIR ATTITUDE AND THEIR HUSTLE</u>.

Tell the kids that given a few breaks, you don't see any reason why you can't compete for the championship, if THEY want to, and YOU do your job right. Very quietly and seriously ask them if they would like to win that championship.

If you don't get a majority of positive responses, you have your work cut out for you, but don't despair. They

may not believe, YET, that they have the ability, or that you can bring it out.

I would suggest that you provide a written contract of sorts to each parent, promising them what you will try your best to do, and what you hope they will do. Here is the contract I am going to give to My kids' parents next season. It's only a point of departure for you, but some sort of understanding with the parents can save a lot of misunderstandings later on.

Dear Mr. and Mrs.

I am genuinely proud to have your child on our team this season. I don't know much about him yet, but look forward to knowing him very well. I hope that by the end of the season I will have made some friends for life, with him, and with your whole family.

On this team, your son will be a winner if he hustles and does his best. Doing his best will involve a few simple commitments. Most of all, he must try always to put the good of his team first. He will be asked to do some things that won't be entirely to his liking at first, but when he sees that I am fair, and care about his individual hopes, he will like them a lot better.

I sometimes talk fairly loudly. I'm partially deaf from flying too much without my hearing protectors, and I never know exactly how to pitch my voice.

I like to tease a lot. If I should accidently hurt your boy's feelings, please accept my apologies now, and please call me at home so I can apologize to him, the next time I see him. If YOU see me doing something you don't understand, or something that you disapprove of, please call me, on the phone, and talk to me.

I hope for the boys to come together as a TEAM, without sacrificing their individuality.

I am going to try to teach them fundamental baseball, and share a heck of a lot of fun doing it.

I will be the loudest cheerer when the boy does HIS best.

Finally, I promise to be the best role model I know how to be, by God's grace.

Thank you

1. Try to get the boys out to the games an hour before starting time.

2. Help your boy by practicing with him and discussing things with him.

3. Check with me if he is going to be absent for a game or practice.

4. All practices will be "RAIN OR SHINE". If it rains we will have "chalk talks" and technique drills under cover.

5. Get your boy to bring a sweat shirt and/or a jacket to practice and to games. It gets cold out here.

6. Come and drag your spouse any time you can. Your cheers are what the kids are working for.

7. On our team, if a boy uses a crude word, he takes a lap. If I use a crude word, I take a lap.

8. If your boy has special needs, please make me aware of it.

My Home phone #   Work phone #

Three final thoughts: first, there are "SPORTS MEDICINE SPECIALISTS" beginning to appear all across the country. If your child is injured, even to the extent of a sore leg or arm, I strongly urge you to ask your family doctor for a referral to one of them. They see sports related injuries every day and may be able to diagnose and treat them with greater clarity and dispatch.

Second, in case you have not already discovered it, there is a wealth of material now available on the subject of "DEVELOPMENTAL TASKS" for pre-adolescent children. I hope you will take advantage of it in learning to communicate with yours.

Finally, I hope you can utilize this season and these games and practices for a vehicle to get involved with your boy. Those tough teen years are in the offing, and every bit of rapport you can muster with him will be money in the bank.

KWB

After handing out your contract, begin asking the kids, starting with the youngest first, where they most like to play. As each one names a position, get them to stand up, get their gloves and pair them off, and show them how to start the ten steps apart "flipping" drill. After you have asked four or five, then start asking for volunteers to play the remaining positions.

When you have filled all nine positions, tell the remaining kids that they are "HITTING GROUP ONE" and tell them to come up with a suitable nick-name for their group, (The Klutzes, The Dribblers, the Stumblebums, or whatever). Get them to introduce themselves to each other, and to remember who they are because they are "hitting group one" for the rest of the season.
(You are building teamlets here.)

While the rest of the kids continue loosening up, have these youngsters grab a bat, and begin your hitting drill by showing them "THE GRIP" and telling them why it is so important. Then show them the "BAT READY POSI-TION" and give them the CUE phrase, "COCK YOUR GUNS NOW."

YOU GOTTA' SELL THIS! There are all sorts of hitting "methods" fads out there, and without any doubt, five years from now there will be a whole different set of flash in the pan fads.

Right now there is a "method" where the kids are supposed to let go of the bat half way through the swing and "dive" onto their front foot. Guess what. That same method got a lot of ink twenty years ago when I was pitching. I loved it. All I had to do was change speeds and watch them hit ground-ball dribblers. Sure was an easy way to pitch nine innings.

The "dive-method" works great off a pitching machine or during batting practice, but an alert pitcher, or catcher, or coach, can make life miserable for a batter who gets caught "drifting" into the pitches.

Now get the fielders to take their positions and have them begin throwing around the infield. Announce to everyone that you are going to play your first game, except that each batter will run on the second hit. The first hit to the infield will be played at first, and a hit to the outfield will be thrown to second. On each batter's second hit, tell them its live baseball, both for the batter/runners and the defense.

Tell your batter/runners to stand still on their team mates' first hit, but to play the second one live.

Rotate "hitting group one" through their batting order TWO times. By this time you will want to have picked "hitting group two". Ask the members of "hitting group one" to fill the positions vacated by "hitting group two". (Have them start the "flipping" drill and warm up drill while you talk to to hitting group two for a few minutes. (You are demonstrating the GRIP and the BAT READY.) Running bases and swinging the bats will have already helped warm up their arms to some degree, but caution them again.

Repeat this rotation through the team roster.

You will want to do a minimum of coaching during this first practice in order to get at least a **feel** for the strengths and weaknesses of each of the players. Take some notes, keeping in mind that they are "rusty" from the off-season.

END the practice by having the youngsters tell you their THREE favorite positions, listed in order with the most favorite first and so on. Write these preferences down by each child's name. SCHEDULE THE NEXT PRACTICE, "RAIN OR SHINE!"

AN EARLY SEASON PRACTICE PLAN

You can save so much time during the course of the season by starting out teaching a few basic "Practice Cues" to get everybody organized. "Give me a circle", might be your cue for your players to form a semi-circle in front of

you so you can demonstrate a particular technique. The "circle" will be as tight as practical for a given demonstration so all the kids can see you.

"Grab your gloves and give me a line" might indicate that you are going to drill them on something...one at a time in sequence, while you watch closely and coach each one.

> Each time you use these "Cues" the first time, explain that it is a cue, and this is what you need them to do when they hear it.

I. Start **all** your practices the same way every time with a progression of throwing drills similar to those outlined in Chapter Four.

II. Then break the kids up into **THREE GROUPS**. One group will be drilling on ground balls, another group will be drilling on catching pop-ups, and the third group will be learning the basics of hitting, (or bunting).

> If you are head coach, you've got to have your assistants get a copy of this book so you are all on the same page. If in fact you are one of the assistants, or an involved parent, get the head coach a copy. He or she will thank you every practice for years to come.

In each of the three groups you will be teaching the essential technique components outlined in the earlier Chapters. Rotate the kids through all the groups each practice, and you take a different group each practice.

FLY BALL GROUP: Here you will want to use soft baseball look-alikes early on, especially for kids ten years old and under. Move the kids back 60 or 70 feet, **always call a name**, and then throw the ball. Teach each child to yell "I want it, I want it" every time as the ball goes into the air. (See Chapter Four.)

GROUND BALL GROUP: Have one of the kids **throwing** the ground balls from about 70 feet. Rotate the throwers. You are next to the ball catchers, showing and telling: Cues: "CHARGE", "DIP", "REAR DOWN", "GLOVE VERTICAL", "CATCH IT BETWEEN YOUR KNEES", "HOP AND SKIP", (for the throw), etc.

During this drill you will want to point out very carefully the difference between "THE INFIELD TECH-NIQUE", (CHARGE, DIP, AND GUN IT), and the "OUTFIELD TECHNIQUE", (not so much charging, but stopping the ball FOR SURE!)

Explain that the infielders always have a back-up, and that they must get to a ball quickly in order to beat a runner with a throw. Then explain carefully that when playing the outfield, the crucial issue is keeping the ball in front of them.

HITTING GROUP: This is where you want to use the "SOFT TOSS DRILL." It's the best drill I've ever found to instill the proper hitting techniques with the kids.

Before you start the drill though, get the group into the semi-circle and demonstrate the elements of great hitting, **in this order:**

1. THE STANCE

2. THE STRIDE

3. BODY ENGLISH

4. HEAD IN

Now break, and let each child take enough swings to firmly memorize these whole-body moves before you go on the the "bat handling" elements. Rotate them through a batting order, two or even three times, showing and "Cueing."

Now demonstrate

5. THE GRIP..."POINTY KNUCKLES"

6. THE BAT-READY..."COCK YOUR GUN"

7. THE WRIST ROLL..."THROW THE PUNCH... CRACK THE WHIP"

Rotate the kids twice through the order again with enough swings to get comfortable with the 7 elements together.

So far there have been **no** baseballs involved at all. We've simply been creating some muscular memories. Now begin the "soft toss drill", coaching, and reminding with the "Cues."

Have your hitting group hitting into a net or into the backstop if possible so you don't have to chase the hit balls, and wiffle balls work pretty well if you don't have a screen.

ANOTHER PRACTICE PLAN

Again break the kids up into their three groups, (hitting groups one, two, and three work well for all these drills so just go ahead and use these groupings.) The following drills work very well together on the same field, which is why I have put them in the same practice.

BUNTING GROUP: In this drill you need a pitcher on the mound and a catcher behind the plate as well. Bunts don't work off the soft toss.

Teach the bunt by going through the steps in chapter two. Some of the kids will probably have been taught "the pivot" to their bunting stance where their feet are in direct line with the pitch.

Break this habit immediately by showing them how unstable they are when trying to bunt an outside pitch, and how vulnerable they are trying to bunt an inside pitch. You want them square to the pitch, arms fully extended, since the only bunt you are going to teach is the "sacrifice bunt" style. (If they are going to bunt for a hit, this style still works best. They just square around a little later. Remind them that they must get the bat on the ball because their runners are moving on the bunt.

BASERUNNING GROUP: Here you will be working on either the lead-off and/or the walking start across the bag, and the "hook-slide" as an intregal part of a steal.

Since you have a pitcher on the mound throwing to the bunters, your baserunners can practice their timing for the break. In addition, you can teach the different kinds of steal. If your kids are ten or older, you want them to be "breaking" on every pitch in a game so get them in the habit here.

You will also be demonstrating again the way to turn a base by using it as a banked turn device, and you will be teaching "game situation awareness" on the bases and throwing in the other base running "sneaky tricks" as they occur to you.

RUNDOWNS GROUP: Using the techniques in Chapter Six, work on the "one throw rundown." Rotate the kids through the three positions in the situation: forward defense player, rearward defense player, and runner. Teach them that a rundown should occur closer to the rearward base. They will get the feel for the situation no other way than to make some of the mistakes they will make during this drill, and it is a lot of fun for everybody. Finally, there is no better drill to gain base running savvy as well as defensive awareness.

SITUATIONS/BATTING PRACTICE

This practice is extremely useful once you have had some several of the teaching practices outlined above. It will

naturally include all of the skills learned early on, and now your kids will get to practice those skills in simulated game conditions. It also gets them used to depending on each other and working as a team.

You and I have both suffered through seemingly endless batting practices where each batter hacked away at a couple of dozen balls while everyone else chased butterflies out of sheer boredom. Not only that, the kids' arms get tired swinging the bat more than eight or ten times in a row and the rest of their practice swings are wasted anyway. Don't let it happen at your practices.

Set up this practice with ground rules similar to those you used in your first practice of the season.

1. Put a pitcher on the mound. Tell him to throw three quarters speed: (a good time to practice "off-speed" pitches.)

2. Always use a catcher.

3. Rotate your hitting groups through the roster two or three times.

4. Play it <u>LIVE</u> on each hitter's second hit, but have every hit played by the fielders.

5. Coach each hitter on The Grip, The Stance, The Bat Ready, The Wrist Roll, The Stride, The Body English, The Head In, and the break from the box.

6. Throw in some bunts.

7. This is also a good time for the kids to practice their base running skills, and for you to watch and coach them.

Finally, station yourself ten feet out of bounds on the third base side for right handed hitters, and out of bounds on the first base side for left handed hitters, and in each case about five steps from the batters. **Keep a couple of balls in your pockets**. No matter how well you are organized, there will be numerous momentary breaks in the action that you can fill with thrown ground balls, thrown pop-ups, and long flys for the outfielders.

INFIELD/OUTFIELD PRACTICE should be just that!

Station your outfielders in back-up positions behind their respective bases before starting infield practice.

1. Hit two rounds softly for a throw to first, coaching them to charge every ball.

2. Hit two rounds for a throw to home, (hit very softly).

3. Hit two rounds for a throw to second, (hit fairly sharply).

4. Two rounds throw to third, (hit fairly sharply).

5. One final round throw to first, (hit fairly softly).

Do you see what we are doing here? We are training the kids to TRY to charge EVERY ball, and we are getting them in the habit of throwing to first on a softly hit ball and to try to get the lead runner on sharply hit balls.

6. Encourage the back-ups/outfielders to complete each play when they get the bad throw during their back-up. Have them run the ball in if they field the overthrow cleanly, and throw out the "runner" at the next base.

THE OUTFIELDERS, should now get two or three rounds of balls while playing their regular position, mixed fly balls and loopers. Tell them where the invisible runner IS! Let them figure out where to throw it. (Remember the "one base-two base" drill? No? Then go re-read the outfielder section.)

THIS WOULD BE A GOOD TIME TO DECIDE HOW YOU WANT TO RUN YOUR CUT-OFF/RELAY PLAYS. WHO IS THE CUT-OFF MAN WHEN GOING TO EACH BASE.

I like to use my first baseman on the right side and my pitcher on the left side for throws to home. (The one not cutting off is the backup.) I use my shortstop from left to second and from left or center to third. Shortstop can also play "deep relay man" from left, with the pitcher as close in cut-off man for a play to the plate.

Play some of these seemingly confusing things during batting/situations practice and they will begin to make sense for the kids. Utilize your first baseman if you can. He will be lonesome after the action has passed his base. Also don't forget a backup for home plate, either the first baseman or the pitcher. The CUE: "WE NEED A CUT-OFF AND A BACK-UP MAN AT _____."

RAINY DAYS should be welcomed by everyone. The parents don't have to wonder if there is practice or not, the kids get together and continue building team spirit, and you can sit them down under cover and have a lot of fun with question and answer chalk talks without the youngsters twitching to hit the field. Get yourself one of those letter size white erase-a-boards with wipe-off markers. DRAW LOTS OF PICTURES.

PRACTICE BEFORE GAMES

I. Batting practice before games is MUCH more important than fielding practice. TRY TO FIGURE OUT HOW TO LET EACH PLAYER HIT TWO OR THREE, TO GET THEIR TIMING ON GAME NIGHT.

(A good way to accomplish that where there is some severe space limitations is to buy some netting approximately fifteen feet long and ten feet high. Cut a rectangular hole in the middle of it just large enough for the batter to see the whole pitcher during his windup when the netting is placed eight feet in front of the temporary home plate. Hanging this netting on some tent poles will create an excellent temporary batting cage.)

II. Start everyone out running a lap to get their blood circulating, then go through the throwing drills.

III. Set the starting pitcher and catcher aside to begin warming up fifteen minutes before game time. ASSIGN A PLAYER TO STAND IN THE BATTER POSITION FOR THE PITCHER/ CATCHER TO GET USED TO! I am convinced that this ploy is crucial. Having been a pitcher, I know that the batter forms the third side of the "frame of reference" for a pitcher.

IV. Designate base coaches and score keepers, (non starters).

V. Give everyone the signals for bunts, steals, etc.

VI. Get everybody together and assign starting positions. Then go through some CUES:

(you)	(kids) (respond)
HIT HARD?	GET THE LEAD RUNNER!
HIT SOFTLY?	GET HIM AT FIRST!
PRIMAL SCREAMS?	ARGGGHHHHHHHH!!!

ETC. (add some of your own)

NEXT THREE BLANK PAGES FOR ADDED "CUES"

CUES AND NOTES

CUES AND NOTES

CUES AND NOTES

PITCHER AND CATCHER PRACTICE

Yes, you are going to pick some of your best athletes to fill these positions. That is all fine and good, but take my advice and look for human traits as well as athletic prowess in making your final decisions. Identify kids who have courage, a willingness to absorb coaching, and the ability to concentrate.

You will probably want to set aside a couple of practices quite early on in the pre-season for your pitchers and catchers only. You are going to want to cover a lot of techniques with them without the distractions of ten other kids running around and needing your attention. Second, you don't want your other players to feel that you are spending too much time with these particular kids.

Set up your pitcher/catcher practice by having everyone take a lap, (about two hundred yards), before allowing them to begin throwing.

Then immediately set up the "flip-it" drill where the kids are only throwing about ten steps. This will cut down on their temptation to fire away before stretching out. Don't let the kids inadvertantly hurt themselves.

Select a pitcher candidate and a catcher candidate, have the catcher don the gear, and sit everyone else down in a group midway between them, (and <u>yes</u>, off to one side). That way your coaching hints will get some repetition and everyone will be better off.

You will thoughtfully have constructed a portable home plate and at least a wooden plank with spikes through it for a pitching "rubber". Make the "rubber" about 18 inches long out of a one by four. The slick surface will only encourage them to pitch off the front **EDGE** of the rubber and that's what you want anyway.

PITCHER CHECKLIST

1. Show your pitchers the pivot. They should begin their windup with their rubber-toe facing directly toward the plate, and complete their throw with their pivot foot side ways to the plate. (They pivot on their TOE! Not their heel!)

2. That pivot foot should be split pretty well down the middle by the front top edge of the rubber as they begin their "controlled fall" toward the plate. (THAT PIVOT FOOT WILL NOW ROLL OVER TOWARD THE PLATE SO THAT THEIR ANKLE IS PERFECTLY STRAIGHT AT THE BALL RELEASE. OTHERWISE THEIR ANKLE WILL BE BENT TO THE SIDE, DESTROYING ANY HOPE FOR PRECISE CONTROL. BENT ANKLES ARE VERY WEAK.)

ANKLE STRAIGHT AT BALL RELEASE

3. By practicing this pivot, and this positioning, it really won't matter what shape any particular mound is in. If there is a hole in front of a rubber it won't hinder your pitchers one bit, and they won't be wallowing around in a hole. The one thing always the same is the front edge of the rubber.

4. The windup is an effort to get up their steam. (Here is that concept, "momentum" again.) Anything that detracts from the effort is wrong.

5. Work toward a gradually acelerating smooth flowing motion directed toward home plate.

6. Make sure your pitchers are "tucking-the-glove". Not only will it make them safer from a line smash, That heavy glove waving around out in the breeze will exert a tremendous leverage upon their body during the delivery, ruining their control potential.

7. Dismiss any type of breaking pitch by explaining that even the best big leaguers couldn't throw a decent curve ball in 46 feet, (youth league pitching distance).

8. Teach three pitches: "the fast-ball", "the off-speed", and "the let up". The off-speed pitch is acomplished by pushing the ball all the way back into the web between the fingers and thumb and throwing it just like a fast ball. He will kill fifteen percent of his velocity and get a lot of ground ball dribblers. The "let up" of course is the old standby. It's a soft arching "watermelon", and is thrown after a fast-ball.

One way to teach the let up is to show the pitchers how to split their two first fingers right around the sides of the ball, all on the white part and throw it just like a fast ball. Some of the older kids will experiment and come up with a wicked "split-finger pitch."

10. Intersperse these two or three pitches a LOT to the top half of the opponents batting order, but stick with fast-balls and off-speed pitches on the bottom half except in all-star play.

11. Stress to your pitchers the value of strong legs. Try to talk them into running stairs two at a time, and/or racing their bicycles around.

12. Get your pitchers in the habit of coming to the plate after any wild pitch.

13. Tell your pitchers, "hit the mitt, over the top, and let her rip!" (Yes, about a zillion times!)

THE FOUR ABSOLUTES OF PITCHING, an article by Dr. Coop De Renne of the University of Hawai and Tom House of the Texas Rangers expresses it best.

I. BALANCE: button of the cap remains directly above the pivot foot until the "weight transfer" begins, (toward the plate). The pitchers accomplish this by bending forward at the hips as they step back to start their wind-up.

II. DIRECTION: lift the knee. Don't kick!

III. WEIGHT TRANSFER: a "controlled fall toward the plate, not a violent shove or push!"

IV. DECEPTION: concealing the ball properly by hiding it in the glove and THEN behind the glove-arm during the delivery is tantamount to moving the pitching rubber FOUR FEET CLOSER TO THE PLATE! Your pitcher hides the ball behind the glove-arm simply by keeping the glove-arm elbow very high during his controlled fall.

CATCHER CHECKLIST

1. Demonstrate the "Squat", with heels off the ground for empty base play.

2. Demonstrate the "FULL CROUCH" for when runners are on base. Teach them to position their feet wider than their shoulders and then squat flat on their heels until the pitcher begins the wind-up. Then they come up so that their thighs are exactly horizontal.

Note how they must lean forward from the hips and extend the mitt to get the low target. The extended arms let them smother a ball better too.

**"THE FULL CROUCH" FOR RUNNERS
ON FIRST OR THIRD**

3. Teach them to offset their "target", and body, inside or outside on every single pitch. Caution them not to exaggerate the offset, but move only six inches to the left and right of center.

See picture on following page.

TARGET OFFSET OUTSIDE ON A
RIGHT HANDED HITTER)

4. "PULL HIM IN", is the <u>CUE</u> for your catchers to adjust their target to one side for a while if the pitcher is missing to the other side consistently.

5. Talk about the foolishness of putting their throwing hand behind them. Show them, **carefully**, how to place it behind the mitt, TOUCHING IT LIGHTLY AND IN A LOOSE FIST.

6. Convince them to throw "SHARP AND FLAT" back to the pitcher every time. See if they can do it while putting down their "catching knee" when in a "Squat." Save them some deep knee bends.

7. Always practice some "Side-arm Flips" from the backstop to the pitcher covering the plate. Position them sideways to the plate and "flip-it" across their odies. This quick release on a passed ball will save a lot of runs.

8. Try to get firmly in their mind not to try to catch a wild pitch in the dirt, but to "smother it" or to block it with their leg and body. *

9. Practice a lot getting them comfortable taking a throw and blocking the baseline for a play at the plate.

10. Coach the "skip and hop" for throwing to second.

11. Teach them to snatch off their mask any time a play is being made, (Except when they are attempting to throw a runner out, of course).

12. Remind them not to turn their head to avoid being hit in the face with a foul tip or wild pitch. The mask has the best protection in front.

EQUIPMENT NOTES:

1. The shin-guards should always be put on with SNAPS faced <u>OUTWARD</u> so your catcher won't be tripping over them.

2. Tell your MALE catchers to wear a pair of jockey briefs under their supporter-cup rig. It will save them some serious CHAFING during the course of a long season.

* SHIFT DRILL

Put a catcher in the gear, have him establish a full crouch stance, and then start TOSSING balls in the dirt to his left and right. THEN GET HIM TO LOCK HIS HANDS BEHIND HIS BACK AND **BLOCK** THE PITCHES, **ON HIS KNEES**, WITH HIS LEGS AND BODY.

CONCLUSIONS AND COACH'S "CUES"

As I sit to conclude this book, I find myself of two minds. I feel a deep sense of satisfaction from having shared with you the fundamentally sound basics of the game, and I feel a particularly poignant sense of loss as well. It's as if you and I have actually spent some time working together with the kids, but now we have to put away the gear and resume our separate lives.

Even as we do so, I believe we can go our separate ways in the firm knowledge that the time spent with the kids is of inestimable value, for them, and for us. For the children because the opportunity to achieve some competency, and perhaps even excellence here, can help lay the foundation for healthy self esteem and self confidence. Perhaps more than anything, a kid needs some "atta-boygurls"!

For us old guys because it furnishes us with a common interest with our sons and daughters; a time for them to teach us how to teach them, and demonstrate our love for them.

There is no question in my mind that you have discovered some of the same things I have, wrestled with some of the same issues I have, and come up with some aids and drills to help that I have not. Nevertheless, I am confident that with this book you can build your relationship with your kids upon trust. Trust that the things you teach them will result in overwhelming success.

I have purposely and consistently cut, and cut, and cut. The refinements and variations on the game have developed for over a hundred years, so my effort here is one of reducing the game to its bare fundamental elements, and presenting them in a clear, terse way.

The book is addressed to you parents and coaches out there, but hopefully one of your kids can pick it up and enjoy it too. I've had a recurring picture in my mind of you and the kids snuggled up in front of a fire on a cold rainy day, waiting for baseball season to begin, and reading this together. If I've accomplished that, the work will have been worth it.

K.W.B.

BATTING CUES:

"COCK YOUR GUN!"

weight on back foot,
bat ready, rear elbow
UP!

"ROLL THOSE WRISTS"

roll wrists during
practice swings

"HEAD IN!"

don't overswing,
but watch the bat hit
the ball, dead center

"GOOD CUT, THOSE
SWINGS MAKE HITS!"

don't fuss about
swings at bad pitches
the kid is either
going to be up there
to hit, or to walk.

"YOU HAVE TO JUMP
ON IT!"

your batter is swing-
-ing late.

"NOW YOU'RE ON IT!"

your batter swung
through the pitch,
but missed.

"YOU'VE GOT TO GUARD
THE PLATE NOW! YOU
ARE ON DEFENSE!"

he has two strikes
and must at least
foul off any pitch
close enough to hit

BASE RUNNING CUES

"SLIDE RIGHT!
HOOK SLIDE RIGHT!"

on a close play at home, tell him as he passes third.

"TWO OUTS, BE RUNNING ON EVERY PITCH!"

always remind runners of the number of outs with advice.

"RONNIE, BE ALERT! ONE OUT NOW!"

always call runner's name before giving them a signal.

"TURN THE BASE! TURN THE BASE!"

always have your runners over run a base ten or fifteen feet if <u>NO</u> play is being attempted on <u>that runner</u>.

"HALF WAY ON A POP-FLY!

on a ball that will "probably" be caught

"TAG ON A DEEP FLY!"

they need to tag-up and be ready to run

ADD SOME OF YOUR OWN CUES

PITCHING AND THROWING CUES

"THROW IT FLAT GUYS! NO BIRD-KILLERS!"

don't allow high looping throws

"FIRE IT OR FLIP IT. NO LOBS!"

encourage sharp throws unless they are close enough to "flip" it.

"SKIP AND HOP, GUYS!"

encourage preparation for the good throw.

"NO <u>DUMB</u> THROWS,GUYS!"

rallys usually get started on a couple of rushed throws or throwing errors

"CATCHER, HELP HIM!"

remind your catcher to <u>pull</u> the pitcher in or to talk to him

FIELDING CUES

"CRASH OR CHARGE?"	response required: "CHARGE! get them to charge every ball unless its a smash.
"OUT FIELD, WHERE'S THE LEAD RUNNER?"	if caught, throw one base ahead of him, if missed, two bases ahead.
"INFIELD..." "HIT HARD?"	(response: "GET THE LEAD RUNNER!"
"HIT SOFTLY?"	(response: "GET HIM AT 1ST!)

Coach, don't hesitate to add to the list or change it to your own clearer words. Have a lot of fun this season, and please write and tell me about any thoughts, techniques, or discoveries you have made to make the game even better a reflection of the best in the American experience.

Again, Thanks
K.W.B.